AN AFTERNOON IN SUMMER

To Aiden and Tris –
Akaperepere au ia korua.

An Afternoon in Summer

Kathy Giuffre

AWA PRESS

First published in 2010 by Awa Press,
16 Walter Street, Wellington, New Zealand

National Library of New Zealand Cataloguing-in-Publication Data
Giuffre, Katherine Anne.
An afternoon in summer : my year on a South Sea island, doing
nothing, gaining everything, and finally falling in love / by
Katherine Giuffre.
ISBN 978-0-9582916-8-2
1. Giuffre, Katherine Anne—Travel—Rarotonga (Cook Islands)
2. Rarotonga (Cook Islands)—Description and travel. I. Title.
919.62304—dc 22

Cover design by Sarah Maxey, Wellington
Typeset by Jill Livestre, Archetype, Wellington
Printed by Everbest Printing Company, China
This book is typeset in Janson Text

www.awapress.com

Produced with the assistance of

ARTS COUNCIL OF NEW ZEALAND TOI AOTEAROA

ABOUT THE AUTHOR

Kathy Giuffre was born and raised in Arkansas, and received a Bachelor of Arts from Harvard University and a PhD from the University of North Carolina at Chapel Hill. She is a professor of sociology at Colorado College and author of *Collective Creativity: Art and Society in the South Pacific.* She lives in Colorado Springs with her husband and two sons.

Come slowly – Eden!
Lips unused to Thee –
Bashful – sip thy Jessamines –
As the fainting Bee –

Reaching late his flower,
Round her chamber hums –
Counts his nectars –
Enters – and is lost in Balms.

EMILY DICKINSON

PREFACE

For *almost a year* I lived at the edge of the ocean, in an old white house with a garden. Sometimes crabs would come up from the beach, find their way into the kitchen and make a tremendous amount of noise, rattling around at night. Sometimes the electricity would go off and we would hunt in the dark for dry matches and go to bed by candlelight. Wild chickens roamed through our garden at dawn and the roosters would crow underneath our windows and wake us up, and sometimes the hens would have a clutch of tiny new chicks with them. Mostly we lived under a hot blue tropical sky but some days it rained all day, from sun up until sundown and on through the night. Once we almost had a hurricane. Two years after we left, four hurricanes hit the island in five weeks and a lot of places that we had known, such as Trader Jack's, were destroyed. Our house was damaged too, but it is an old, strong house and it is still standing.

I lived there with my two children. Aiden was seven when we arrived and Tris was three. Their father had left when I was pregnant the second time, so it seemed as though it had always been just the three of us. It didn't seem strange to be living on an island so far away from everything we knew, as long as we were together.

Rarotonga is the main island of the Cook Islands, a country in central Polynesia, west of Tahiti and east of Tonga. Tiny and beautiful, it is surrounded by a wide turquoise lagoon and a sharp coral reef. I had a modest grant to study artists there. My contact in the prime minister's office had lined up a new house for us and had set me up with an "associate researcher".

Some of my friends in the US thought I was crazy to pack up my children, leave everything else behind, and head off to a place I'd never been before, a place with dengue fever and elephantiasis and dysentery, just because I liked the sound of it. Maybe. But even now, years later, part of me still lives in our old white house on the edge of the sea.

I had been alone ever since Eric, the boys' father, had left. I was numb from exhaustion. I had, after all, two small children—babies. If you have just one small child, you know this child will have to sleep sometime and that you will sleep then. You may not shower for weeks on end or brush your teeth or even comb your hair, but you will sleep. However, once you are outnumbered with two small children it is possible they will engage in tag-team sleeping so that at least one of them is always awake.

I loved my children. Nevertheless, it was hard raising them by myself. They needed so much from me—every spoonful of food, every bath, every diaper change, every lullaby, every game of peek-a-boo, every piece of laundered clothing, every washed dish, every kiss, every bandage, every everything. Sometimes I would see other mothers hand a child to its father and marvel, wide-eyed and longing, like a prisoner looking at the sky.

Once the boys got a bit older and I wasn't their whole world, the real problems began. Now I was their only protection from the *other* world—the one of slings and arrows. The outside world seemed full of people with trumped-up excuses to explain why they were bad-tempered—people like Aiden's first-grade teacher, who told the children she had Cherokee blood and that was why she would never smile. How could I protect my children every moment of every day—even when I was at work and they were far away—from the casual heartlessness of other people? How could I be everything and everywhere at once? Would I ever have anything approaching a "normal" life again? I was worn out from trying.

I didn't die, as I feared, but I didn't have any offers of romance either. This may have been because I was tired, miserable and hadn't showered in weeks. I became sadly resigned to a future without men.

But then one day there was Gregg. It's the old story. There you are, blithely playing with fire, and the next thing you know things have got out of hand—got out of hand even though you know full well he has a girlfriend. He tells you it's over, he hasn't loved her in years. He never loved her, not really. The two most dangerous words in the English language: "Only you." Gregg may as well have been holding up a sign that said, "Today's special—Heartbreaks half-price". I would have rushed over with my credit card.

At the time, the world seemed a complicated, entangled morass. Not only was there the matter of Aiden's teacher but my colleagues at work were entrenched in internecine warfare, the American people had just elected a frighteningly stupid man as president, and Gregg's girlfriend seemed inexplicably unwilling to disappear. I just wanted to get away. The idea was that Gregg and the boys and I would go to the South Seas together. We would be alone, far away, on an island in the sun, free of all the complications and entanglements. It was only later it occurred to me that as far as Gregg was concerned there was really just one entanglement, and he could have walked away from her any time he chose.

As a professor, I was entitled to a sabbatical every seven years—a year without teaching or other duties, during which I was supposed to work on research. My sabbatical year was coming up and it seemed perfect timing. I applied for a grant to study the indigenous art of Rarotonga and was successful. Things were falling into place. Then, ten days before we were scheduled to leave, Gregg told me he wasn't coming.

ARRIVAL

Wednesday, July 31
Arrived paradise stop
beautiful beyond our wildest
dreams stop
have eaten no dog stop
yet
stop

I*t was late July* when Aiden, Tris and I left Colorado with a suitcase full of shorts and summer dresses for the flight first to Los Angeles and then on to Tahiti, where we waited to reboard our plane in the dark, echoing airport. Finally at two in the morning we touched down in Rarotonga. It is thrillingly terrifying to land in the dead of night at a strange foreign airport with no one you know to meet you and no idea what will happen next. Rarotonga was such a brief stopover for the plane on its way to Auckland that it had not even been mentioned at the gate at Los Angeles international airport.

Here it was a much bigger deal. A man was playing the ukulele and singing on a small stage in the terminal to welcome the plane's arrival. It was too dark to see the ocean, but even from the front of the airport I could hear it. Although it was the middle of the southern winter there seemed to be flowers everywhere. Sleepy-looking people from the hotel threw leis around our necks. Tris twisted his double and put it on his head, looking a little like Julius Caesar. There were also lizards; I would learn that these "moko" ran around near lights at night and ate bugs.

I stood on the sidewalk by our suitcase, holding Aiden with one hand and Tris with the other, waiting to be loaded on to the van that would take us to our hotel, and tried to realise that this was real, tried to hear the ocean and smell the flowers and impress this moment into my brain forever—the moment when we arrived.

First thing next morning, I called the number I had been given for Mr Tarau, the man who would be renting us a house. He wasn't there. Then for most of the rest of the day the phones were out. It was the same the next day. To make matters worse my only government contact turned out to have left the country on the out-bound flight of the plane that had brought us in. With a feeling of impending doom, I extended our stay at the hotel. "How many more days?" the pretty girl at the desk asked. "Only two," I said, faking optimism.

The truth was that things had started off badly—so badly, in fact, that it was only about a week before I decided to give it all up. I would repack our bags, change our return tickets, take my boys in my arms, and drag my pitiful self to ... where? There were already tenants living in our house in Colorado. And I didn't want to go back there anyway. Not there.

The days crawled by with no sign of Mr Tarau, or of anyone else with whom I had been in contact from the US. If the island was not exactly deserted, it was at least devoid of the people who had assured me, before our arrival, of their aid and their interest. There was no house for us, it seemed. And no working phones and no help any-where—only cool, beautiful faces with eyes that flicked across me impassively. I could be a ten-day tourist—that was the usual procedure—but the only response to my intention to stay on the island was an uncomprehending blankness.

I was quickly running over budget living in the Grand Beachfront Suite of the Rarotongan Beach Resort and Spa, which I had meant to be a two-night treat but which had turned into a pecuniary folly. I was also running out of patience trying to keep my jet-lagged little boys quietly entertained from four in the morning, when they woke up, until seven, when the hotel restaurant opened for break-fast. It didn't seem wise to take them out on to the cold and wind-scoured beach in the dark, so I futilely tried to keep them from screaming, taking to heart the disgrun-tled "Goddamn it!" I had heard through the apparently tissue-thin wall of our room on the second morning. After three hours of whispered threats and grouchy despair, it was hideous to discover that not only was there not a house for me after all but, according to everyone I spoke to, it was very difficult to find a house to rent on the island. I should keep my eyes on the classifieds in the paper—a house might pop up some day. Having given me this advice, no one really gave a damn. Who cared about one lost gringa and her two noisy children? Sell her some T-shirts and send her on her way.

But not only could I not bear the thought of going back to Colorado, I couldn't imagine any other place on the surface of the globe that I *could* bear the thought of. I just wanted oblivion, and as they say in Arkansas, you can't get there from here.

It's relatively easy to be breezy and nonchalant when discussing casually among your colleagues at work—especially ones you don't like—the possibility that for your sabbatical you will fly off to spend a year in the South Seas. "West of Tahiti" is a lovely phrase to say to people who are so timorous and moribund they won't even eat sushi.

And having uttered not only "west of Tahiti" but also "Rarotonga", "indigenous artists" and "International Date Line", you would be surprised how quickly you can find yourself applying for grant money, and being given the necessary permissions and waivers and forms from the health insurance company. I was suddenly in email contact with Te Aturangi Tamarua in the Office of the Prime Minister of the Government of the Cook Islands, trying to write in Māori out of a phrasebook, "My son has broken his arm on the playground" and instead writing, "The arm they are cutting an area of games looks like my son." I asked for help with the house, though, in English. Or now that I think about it, I never asked—Te Aturangi Tamarua offered. "Would you like me to get a house for you?" "Yes," I responded, happy to find this was all as easy as I was making it sound in my collegial conversations. "Te Aturangi Tamarua" is almost as nice to say as "west of Tahiti". Maybe nicer.

And nice Te Aturangi Tamarua gave me another name: Mr Tarau. He had a house for me. I was to call when we landed. Everything was taken care of.

Only it wasn't. I couldn't find Mr Tarau and nice Te Aturangi Tamarua had gone away and I was running out of money and patience and sanity and ideas. Hence the despair: I was stunned—*shocked*—by what I had actually done.

I sent perky postcards to everyone on my mailing list, was stalwart and soothing—in a cranky German-governess sort of way—for the sake of the boys, and only barely admitted, even to myself, that things might not be quite perfect here in paradise. Having come to the South Seas on a dare that no one except me even knew I'd taken,

I couldn't very well send out a mass email begging for rescue, and admit to all those well-meaning friends who had cautioned me that I was about to make a big mistake that I had, in fact, made a big mistake.

It is possible, of course, that seeing myself as the heroine of a romantic palm-fringed adventure, I assumed that other people did too, and seriously overestimated the degree to which anyone, other than my father, thought about me at all. But the effect of an audience is remarkable, no less for being imaginary. While I was carefully composing in my head the postcards that would turn them all green with envy and me into a modest legend, they were probably saying to themselves, "I wonder if Kathy has left for her trip yet? Where was she going again? Can't remember. Oh, well, shall we have tacos for dinner?"

Of course there was Gregg—the one other person in the world besides my father who was, I was certain, thinking about me. And it was of some necessity that he should writhe—absolutely *writhe*—with envy. I wanted him to regret what he had lost as much as I did. I had lost him, but I couldn't seem to leave him behind. In one of those sadistic jokes that the gods like to play, the only brand of instant coffee available on Rarotonga had turned out to be called "Gregg's"—even spelled his way, with three gs. Every morning a fresh batch of Gregg's was delivered to my hotel room, every restaurant table had a stack of Gregg's packets in a glass container in the centre, and I couldn't go into the grocery store without seeing him everywhere.

Of course, Gregg was on my email list because cool modern women never ever hold grudges, but there was no point in sending out an electronic SOS when the only person I wanted to rescue me would, I knew, never come. Better to continue on. And there was this: however much sorrow I felt over Gregg, sorrow that ran through my blood like an insidious poison, part of me was still fucking furious. I wanted him to die, painfully, of prolonged regret or, better yet, chainsaw wounds. And while he was dying—lingeringly, to give him time for contemplation—I wanted him to imagine me happy, laughing and uproarious in my exotic paradise.

During the day it was windy at the beach, which we had to ourselves. Aiden couldn't swim because just before we left he had broken his arm and now had a cast on it, so he would just wade out up to his waist, which was chest-high for Tris. Then they would wade back together and play for a while in the sand. They seemed very small under such a big sky. I would sit on the empty sand and stare out at the line of breakers that marked the reef and try to come up with Plan B.

Mr Tarau was never at his office when I called, during those fleeting moments when the phones were working.

"When will he be in?" I would ask. "Oh, later," his secretary would say. Finally, after three days—thinking that maybe I would track him down in person—I asked, "Where is he *right now*?" "New Zealand," she said. "Ah," I said, somewhat deflated, "when do you expect him back?" "Oh," she said airily, "later. Maybe next week. Or the week after that. Later."

Despite living in an air-conditioned hotel room, it still seemed very adventurous to be on Rarotonga, as though we were characters in a Joseph Conrad novel, or Fletcher Christians in a remake of *Mutiny On The Bounty*. The real mutiny had, indeed, happened just nearby, when the *Bounty* was transporting breadfruit tree saplings from Tahiti to the West Indies, where the starchy fruit was meant to be used as a cheap source of food for African slaves. After the mutiny, the sailors had thrown the saplings overboard and set Captain Bligh adrift in a small open boat. The real irony was that when, a few years later, another ship did manage to get breadfruit trees to the West Indies, the slaves vehemently refused to eat the breadfruit. They preferred to starve.

I had always found this strange until the first day in Rarotonga, sitting at a table in the Te Vaka Restaurant at the Rarotongan Beach Resort and Spa, having piled my plate with tropical delicacies at the buffet, I put a big chunk of breadfruit in my mouth. Because the boys were watching me expectantly and because I'd been so chirpy about trying new things, I did manage to swallow it and I did manage to smile, but it brought tears to my eyes, and not ones of joy.

In the empty afternoons of waiting we went for long walks down the beach, never seeing another human soul. It wasn't tourist season and the local people considered sunbathing to be evidence of stunning ignorance (when they were feeling charitable), or stunning stupidity (when they weren't). One day, we came across some very large starfish sitting in the shallow water. They were an intense deep velvet blue. Tris wanted to bring them home with us and was sad to leave them behind. "Bye-bye, my little ocean friends," he said.

Despite the lack of all human contact other than waitresses, Aiden quickly began picking up island culture. On our third day he swallowed a bug by accident. "It just flew straight into my mouth," he said. "What do you suppose it did that for?" I asked. "I don't know," he said solemnly. "Maybe it was sacrificing something to one of its gods."

Finally, after spending two months' worth of my budgeted money in one week at the resort, I pulled myself together enough to realise that even if there was no house, or hope of one, we could at least move to a cheaper hotel. I went to the prime minister's office and roamed around plaintively, with the boys making sad doe-eyes behind me, until someone—not the still-missing Te Aturangi

Tamarua, whom in the end I never did meet—said, "Why don't you ring Malcolm at the Central Motel? That's where we always put" [delicate pause] "people."

Malcolm was jolly over the telephone.

"I hope you can help me," I began.

"Oh, I hope so too!" he smiled: he was the sort of person you could hear smiling over the phone. He would be delighted to have us join him at the Central Motel. He would pick us up in front of the Rarotongan Beach Resort and Spa at ten o'clock the next morning.

I began to have hope again—a smiling man from the other end of the telephone was coming tomorrow to save us! I herded the boys back to the hotel to pack our suitcase, eat one last meal of hamburgers and French fries in the Te Vaka Restaurant, and have one last hilarious bubble bath in the en suite Jacuzzi. After I put the boys to bed for one last air-conditioned sleep in the Grand Beachfront Suite, I drank two beers from the minibar and sat in the solitary pool of bedside lamplight feeling relieved. The intolerable stasis of waiting had cracked. After a week of feeling we hadn't really got off the plane, it seemed we had at last begun to arrive.

Many years ago I came close to marrying a man named Alvis. He and I spent a weird night in a town on the eastern coast of Guatemala. The town was inaccessible by road: the only way to get there was in an open canoe down a wide river. The town itself had fewer than a hundred people; it was some sort of failed United Fruit Company idea. By the time we turned up it was a miserable flea-and-mosquito-infested hellhole with muddy streets and sickly chickens.

Right on the edge of the ocean there was a magnificent white hotel. It had been built with misguided Arab oil money and was kept fully staffed and gorgeous, despite the fact there had been few guests for years. Alvis and I checked in. The first night a torrential storm blew in from the ocean, and we sat in the bar getting drunk with the lonely bartender and a bunch of garrulous exotic birds that had been set free from their cages on the hotel's ornamental lake so they wouldn't get drowned in the storm. The bar had no walls, only wooden blinds that we tried to lash down enough to keep out the worst of the gale. There was no electricity and we drank warm beer by the light of a hurricane lantern. It was probably the most beautiful bar I've ever seen.

The storm died down around sunrise and we went to sleep. Later I woke with a raging fever that went higher and higher, until finally I was delirious and Alvis had to leave me alone and try to find a doctor. There wasn't a doctor of course, but he managed to scrounge some expired penicillin that got me well enough to travel all the way back to Guatemala City, and gave me a permanent allergy to penicillin. Because of the storm and the beers and the fever, my memories of the town are hazy and dreamlike, but strangely I have loads of photos: me, very pale, by the edge of the hotel's pristine swimming pool; Alvis laughing with the ocean roiling behind him.

During the first lost days on Rarotonga, those images —the empty hotel, the bar, the wind-driven rain—kept coming into my mind. The huge deserted hotel and the loneliness of the storm had made it seem that Alvis and I had come to the end of the world. Now Rarotonga seemed like that too, an island at the end of the world. Maybe it was because of the vastness of the sea, beyond human understanding.

Malcolm, just as unflappable in person as he had been on the phone, came the next morning and loaded our explosion of luggage, beach balls, bags of laundry, wet bathing suits, extra snacks and hyperactive boys into his white van. He was clearly a man of immense kindness because I was no prize, even as a paying guest. I don't mean physically, although I had certainly reached the state of sweaty red blotches that white women often achieve after a week in the tropics. I mean emotionally, because on top of being a sopping, heartbroken mess, I hadn't yet learned how to calm down, how to go with island time, how to let things come as they will. I kept wanting things to *happen*, and for the children to *behave well*, and for the clothes to fit back in the suitcase they came out of. I wanted things to work the way they were supposed to work, and if they weren't working I wanted someone, somewhere, to do something. Now.

Malcolm, on the other hand, was an old hand at island time. He was an English refugee who had been on the island for decades. Not long ago I read a book of travel essays, set on various islands around the South Pacific, in which Malcolm is mentioned by name. The writer made fun of Malcolm's name and his accent and his penchant for alarmingly attractive women. It was an unkind description, and made me dislike the writer personally and intensely. I especially disliked him because Malcolm himself had recommended another of his books and I had bought it and read it and thought it awful tripe, but by that point I had already enriched the writer by buying his book. And he had never done a damn thing for me, other than taking my money and boring me for an afternoon, whereas Malcolm had scooped up my children and me from the Rarotongan Beach Resort and Spa and saved my sorry ass from despair.

The Central Motel turned out to be a two-storey building enclosing a pocket-sized courtyard of lush green tranquillity a hundred yards off the main road in the centre of Avarua. Avarua is the capital of the Cook Islands, and just as Jane Austen characters refer to London as "Town", Rarotongans call Avarua "Town". Unlike eighteenth-century London, however, Avarua is really only one street, three blocks long, with the ocean on one side and a smattering of shops on the other. As well as being the only place, other than the airport, with an ATM, it is the hub of two buses that slowly circle the island each hour—one going clockwise, one going anti-clockwise on a road following the beach. There are a handful of restaurants and fried chicken takeaways, government offices, a doctor's surgery, and two benches for sitting on while staring out at the rusted remains of an ancient wreck at the mouth of the harbour.

Rarotonga itself is shaped like a slightly squashed circle, with a narrow band of level land at the shore and steep, jungle-covered mountains in the middle. It is too breathtaking to be pretty, but is beautiful in the way that things can be only if they have something dark hidden in their depths. At the very foot of the mountains there is a road built a thousand years ago by an ancestor called Toi. Although the road peters out all together in some places, you have to follow it if you want to find the sites of ancient marae, the sacred temples where the Rarotongans worshipped their gods for a millennium before the Christian missionaries came and moved everyone out to the beach, where the missionaries could see clearly what was going on.

In Town a few streets lie perpendicular to the main road running inland for a few blocks, and if you walk along them you can suddenly come to a giant mango tree that has dropped all its green fruit on to the roadway to rot, or a lone cow standing undisturbed in the shade of a frangipani tree, or a small shop called the Perfume Factory with a monkey named Lulu in an elaborate cage outside. For now we lived in Town.

Waiting for the elusive Mr Tarau to come back from New Zealand was starting to wear thin. It is surprisingly hard to live incessantly in a hotel or motel. I made friends with Nga, who cleaned the rooms. She didn't clean our room any more—there was no point. Instead, she and I would sit for a while in the mornings and talk. She had eight children and was surprised and sorry for me that I had only two. She told me that sometimes she left the children at home when she went to church so she could get a little peace and quiet. She asked me right away where my husband was. Then she patted my arm compassionately and told me not to worry—there was someone else out there for me. We would talk until the boys started to climb the walls and then I would leave and take them to the park next to the market, or to the beach or the library, or to run errands with me.

There were three grocery stores on the island. The big one was the CITC. The grocery bags said "Cook Islands Trading Company—Since 1891". A book in my house has a picture of the interior of the CITC in 1943. Dark-skinned women in white hats and white dresses mingle with fish hooks and Gillette razor blades. Tins of cabin bread are stacked on shelves behind glass-topped counters. There's one guitar, one badminton racquet, and "Boss" McKegg, the owner, standing in the dusty light, a pale lion in his own domain, his white shirt shining ghost-like in the gloom. In a shack out the back they stored the bags of copra taken in trade.

These days the store was a sort of warehouse just outside town. It was filled with cartons of canned mackerel from Japan, but still seemed somehow empty. The groceries had the air of having ended up there because they had been left on the boat by accident when it made its other stops—stops at real places with real streets and real shops and brightly lit grocery stores filled with real, high-quality groceries. Mostly, the CITC sold canned goods and ramen noodles. There was also a cold room where dairy products and fresh vegetables were kept. This was nice and cool, and when I came back out into the rest of the store my glasses would fog up.

The grocery store right in town was called Foodland. It was smaller than the CITC and less empty. It seemed less friendly though, maybe because it was busier. There were always one or two shattered-looking honeymoon tourist couples disconsolately buying two-litre bottles of water from the tall stack near the front door, a sure sign they had developed stomach problems from drinking tap water. On the other side of the island was Wigmore's Superstore. Mr

Wigmore's grandiosity seemed to have been completely exhausted in coming up with the name. The store was almost, but not quite, as big as a decent-sized American convenience mart. It too was semi-empty, but it did have some big baskets of produce sitting in the middle of the floor. There was a basket of taro and a basket of taro leaves, called "rukau" when they are cooked. There were paw-paws, and sometimes tomatoes or watermelons. There were fresh-baked baguettes, and we could buy the local newspaper and some travel-worn English candy bars from a cooler against the back wall.

Sometimes we would buy food at one of the stores and eat sandwiches in our room or at the beach, but mostly we ate at the Maitai Café in the centre of town—where wild chickens aggressively hunted for food scraps under, and occasionally on, the tables—or at the Blue Note Café, which was part of a building called the Banana Court. This had been the Hotel Rarotonga when there was only one hotel on the island, and then for a while a "banana court" had been held there to settle disputes about agricultural exports, mostly bananas. Our guide-book optimistically called Banana Court "once the best known drinking hole and dance hall in the Cook Islands, indeed in the whole South Pacific ... still a major land-mark". It didn't seem all that major any more, or maybe just not in the warm afternoons when we went there to while away a long late lunch. There were sometimes one or two tourists eating and leafing through the fantastically out-of-date collection of old magazines and New Zealand newspapers, but that was about it. There were two nice women, one cooking and one waiting tables and running the cash box. Both would come out to the table to take our order.

"Here's the big man!" the cook would say, lifting Tris up into his chair. "How's my big man today?"

We ate ika mata—raw fish marinated in lime juice and coconut cream. Aiden, especially, loved it, but I had a dream one night that I was eating a barbecue sandwich.

I grew up in Arkansas, in the same faded town where my mother and her mother and her mother's mother had grown up. In a sixth-grade classroom I had planted the seeds of my year in the South Seas. I was bored, browsing in the back of the classroom on a dusty shelf where books were kept on the slim chance that some freakish child might some day want to read something. I wish now that I had a copy of the book I found, a child-appropriate retelling of Margaret Mead's research in Samoa. Stripped of all the enticing depictions of sybaritic sex that had made Mead the world's first anthropological celebrity, it was the story of a young woman going off to Polynesia to be paddled around in canoes, sleep in thatched huts, dance, and write a book about it. "This is a *job*?" I said to myself. Who knew?

My parents, supportive of my new career goal, rousted up the son of a friend of a friend who was an actual anthropologist and took me to meet him for dinner when he came to Arkansas to visit his parents. He obligingly entertained me with gruesome stories of having to eat live monkey brains and other local delicacies, which put me off anthropology for a while, but as I got older I mastered raw oysters, straight bourbon, caviar, pâté, calamari, eel sashimi, Roquefort cheese, escargot and sperm. And really, considering the hygiene of some former boy-friends, how bad could monkey brains be?

So now—almost thirty years later—I was living on an island in Polynesia, supposedly to study the indigenous artists. Two days after we arrived at the Central Motel a woman named Elise called me, alerted to my where-abouts by the island gossip network that had been, un-beknownst to me, tracking my every move. Elise had been assigned to me as "associate researcher" by the Research Committee of the Cook Islands Government's Founda-tion for National Research, in reality half a back room in a temporary Quonset hut on an unused patch of ground near the prime minister's office. She gave me a breathless rundown of all the artists on the island and their feuds and friendships and other affairs. The interrelationships seemed Byzantine and I had a hard time following her torrent of information, not helped by Aiden and Tris seiz-ing the opportunity of my being tied up on the telephone to dance around madly just out of arm's reach, bopping each other with pillows and battling delightedly near delicate glass table lamps and cups of scalding hot tea.

Undeterred, Elise invited me to go with her the following week to the opening of a group show. It was to be at an art gallery in a village called Arorangi. She would introduce me to some of the artists who had provided me with a convenient excuse to be here.

Because moving to a place in another hemisphere where you have never been before and don't know anyone or anything is not challenging enough for a single mother of two, Aiden had broken his arm in the playground five weeks before we left—hence the cast. The day before we flew out, the orthopaedist decided we should leave Aiden's arm in the cast for the trip and then have the cast removed after we had been on the island for a week or two. It sounded a prudent, sensible idea. Once we were settled in the Central Motel, I set about trying to get the cast removed.

First we tried Dr Kush, an Indian woman with a small surgery behind the bus stop. Malcolm said Dr Kush had been stranded on Rarotonga by her husband when he fell in love with a local girl and moved with her to one of the northern islands. She did seem forlorn, but there may have been other reasons. I thought she eyed the bright-blue high-tech breathable-fibreglass-mesh cast rather uneasily, and when she brought out a pair of what looked like fingernail scissors from her desk drawer and started feebly scratching away at it I knew things were not going to go as I had envisioned them when the doctor in Colorado had decided not to just split the cast and wrap it up for the trip.

After a few minutes of scratching sheepishly, Dr Kush said, "I think you're going to have to go up to the hospital."

The bus didn't go to the hospital. It went to the bottom of a road that led up the side of a mountain. The hospital was on top. We walked and we walked and we walked. "Gosh, Aiden," I said, "it's a good thing you didn't break your leg!" I wondered what you would do if you were, say, bleeding from the head. But we got there eventually, after some gorgeous views out over the ocean.

We were shown into an operating room cum storage shed. Blooming vines pressed hard against the windows outside, and moko hung upside down from the ceiling. The doctor was very nice and, as it turned out, very strong, which was fortunate because there appeared to be nothing on hand capable of cutting through the cast. He pulled out a giant version of Dr Kush's fingernail scissors and started trying to clip. When nothing happened, he climbed up on the examining table with Aiden so he could get better leverage and pushed on the cast-cutter with all his strength. By using his body weight, he was slowly able to make a little progress. At one point, I saw him start to raise his foot up, searching for a better position by bracing it against Aiden's chest, but he saw me eyeing him and thought better of it. "Well, that's it," I thought, feeling like a desperate mother wolf. "I'll just have to *chew* the damn thing off." Finally, though, the doctor, drenched with sweat and flushed with unexpected victory, had hacked Aiden to freedom.

We thanked him a lot and left the hospital to walk home. We didn't have to pay anything because medical care is free for children in the Cooks. They may not have bright-blue high-tech breathable-fiberglass-mesh casts, but it is a truly civilised country.

By moving to town, even though we were still in a kind of hotel, we had left the hermetically sealed confines of the resort and begun to feel we were really living in this new place. The Central Motel also had packets of Gregg's instant coffee in a bowl next to the electric kettle, but I kept forgetting to notice them so much and feel so miserable. I borrowed Malcolm's computer to send an email back to my friends.

Thursday, August 15
Dear everyone,

We are still marooned in a hotel, living on the edge of an everlasting stream of tomorrows.
It is hard to live indefinitely this way; we entertain ourselves as best we can and wait for our life here to

really begin. I took the boys to see "Spirit: Stallion Of The Cimarron" last Friday night at the Empire Cinema—the only movie theatre in the country, conveniently located 200 yards from our hotel. During the intermission (while the reels were being changed in the projector—how strangely reminiscent of grade-school health films the clicking whirr of a projector is ...) I saw something coming across the floor towards us. "My," I thought to myself, "what a brave mouse."

It was a cockroach. I did not point it out to Aiden, who doesn't perhaps fully appreciate the amazing growth capacity of the local cockroaches. Tris has it worse—he has discovered a deep-seated fear of wild chickens. This is unfortunate as a gang of outlaw roosters roams the street in Avarua (our village) with much the same attitude as Marlon Brando in "The Wild Ones". They are very surly, but—as I tell the boys—I have a Swiss Army knife and a recipe for chicken stew. I wait for my chance.

It's interesting to live someplace where almost everything comes by ship and the ships come across hundreds of miles of unpredictable ocean. Currently, the entire country is out of natural gas. The boat is late, expected tomorrow, but for the past few days there has been no cooking—not at the restaurants, not at the hotels, nowhere. No amount of *money can buy gas. The boat is late and that is that. The whole country is also out of milk and disposable diapers. We are not out of coconuts. We have plenty. I have been repeatedly warned never to park a car under a coconut tree as a falling coconut can completely take out a Toyota. It makes lazing in a hammock under the palms seem rather more exciting than I had originally envisioned.*

Still no leads on the promised house. One does not mock the Bungalow Gods. Take care.

Love, Kathy

EMILY

Thinking back now it seems that we lived in the Central Motel for a long time, but really it was only about two weeks. We didn't do much other than hang around town or go swimming on the south side of the island, where the lagoon was wide and calm, and where, across the road from the beach, we could buy lunch at a stall called Fruits of Rarotonga, that also sold home-made jams and preserves. We went to the library sometimes and I still have my battered library card. It lists my address as "Central Motel". So does my Cook Islands driver's licence, which I got one Saturday morning at the police station and then went and rented a car, giving us freedom from the once-an-hour bus schedule. We did go to the movies a couple of times, but mostly we moped around the motel, chatting with Nga and Malcolm and waiting for Mr Tarau to come back.

Malcolm knew Mr Tarau, and although he didn't say it I got the strong impression he didn't think much of him. In any event, Malcolm was now on the case, monitoring Mr Tarau's global position. This was done most efficiently from the bar at Trader Jack's right on the edge of the harbour, to which all news on the island was instantly relayed. Consequently, within hours of Mr Tarau's arrival, Malcolm had him on the phone and got directions to the house. We hightailed out to the village of Aroroangi to finally see our long-awaited dream home.

Oh. My. God. On an island almost painful in its beauty, an island for which scores of nineteenth-century British sailors had run the risk of being flogged to death for desertion, an island whose lure had launched at least a thousand ships, an island that had threatened to undermine the missionaries' whole theological edifice because of the distinct suspicion they had somehow stumbled into the prelapsarian Eden, on this island Mr Tarau owned the only ugly house. It was not just a little ugly either. It was a beige cinder-block square stranded in the middle of a treeless yard.

It was a miracle that such a desert wasteland could exist in the midst of the lush oasis surrounding it. Two more units were also being constructed, complete with bulldozers, mud, leering construction workers and sharp, rusty rebar points projecting out of the walls at the exact level of the children's eyes. Inside was actually worse. The house was completely unfurnished, with the exception of some mouldy food left in the kitchen sink by whichever unfortunates had lived there. Two giant cockroaches scavenged for crumbs on the bench.

Mr Tarau arrived a few minutes later, and seemed as unperturbed by the cockroaches as they were by him. Middle-aged and heavy, he managed to seem both terrifically bored and terrifically irritated at the same time.

"I thought it was supposed to be furnished," I said.

"You buy the furniture," he said.

"But what am I going to do with a houseful of furniture when I leave?" I said.

"You can leave it here," he said.

"But furniture is expensive."

"You can buy it little by little." He smiled for the first and only time.

This was the house. The only house. We had waited three weeks for it, and in all that time we had never had as much as a faint lead on any other house.

Another cockroach emerged from the edge of the kitchen bench and scuttled across the surface towards me; there was a disturbing rustling noise from underneath the counter.

"Our things are at the motel," I said, defeated.

"Bring the first month's rent by my office this afternoon," he said.

Even though we drove back to the motel in the car, I felt as though I were trudging.

Malcolm fairly exploded. It was outrageous, he said. Expecting you to furnish his house for him! The swine! Not even clean! The swine! Surrounded by construction! The *swine!*

It was a heartwarming tirade, although, when I think about it now, perhaps the fact my children were still waking up well before dawn and that Malcolm lived through the wall from us may have had something to do with his anxious solicitousness to see us suitably settled down—elsewhere.

While Malcolm was busy exploding in outrage, Nga, who was enjoying the spectacle, suggested to Malcolm that he call Emily.

"I certainly will," Malcolm said huffily. "We'll see about this. Not a stick of furniture—the swine!"

He then miraculously changed voices as the mysterious (neither he nor Nga saw any need to enlighten me) Emily answered the phone.

"Emily, dear? Malcolm here. How are you? Lovely. And Elizabeth? Lovely. Tell her I said hello when you speak to her. Yes.

"Now then, I have a woman here with her two darling children. They're Americans, but they're very nice anyway. And she needs a place—can I send her round to see you? Yes. Now don't put them down in the little house; take them in with you. Yes. Yes. Right away."

Three minutes later the boys and I were back in the car, heading along a road just outside town to a village called Panama. (I later learned it had been named after a wildly disastrous government scheme to harness the power of the tides by digging a canal inland from the beach and letting the water flow in and out and turn a turbine. It did, apparently, seem plausible at the time.)

Emily's house sat back from the road in a glade of trees and flowers. The edges of the garden were bordered by thickets of wild gardenias and hibiscus, and the palm trees overhead were breaking the sunlight into a dappled, murmuring shade. Even though it was close to town, it felt as though we were far away.

We parked under a big frangipani tree and Emily came out on to the veranda to greet us. She was small and fine-boned and old—in her eighties—but lovely, with long iron-grey hair and clear brown eyes. You could tell that in her youth she had been very beautiful. Her voice was quiet and her laughter was like little silver bells.

I felt shy and awkward; it had occurred to me stupidly and belatedly that with Emily we wouldn't have a house, only a room in a house, which wasn't what I wanted at all. Emily took me slowly around the house, and stopped in the soft light of the kitchen window to show me a picture of her daughter, Elizabeth, who looked like a younger version of Emily. She was wearing a white nun's habit.

"You're Catholic?" I asked. "Yes," she said, looking at me hesitantly.

"We're Catholic, too," I said, neglecting to mention it had been years since I'd graced a church.

She smiled at me, and our eyes stayed locked for one moment too long for people who are strangers. Out of all the jumbled images and memories that I have of those days, that one moment is clear, like a photograph in my mind—a photograph that I can feel and smell and hear, as well as see. In that moment of stillness I can see, even now, the slate-blue afternoon light in the kitchen, feel the warmth of the children standing close to me, and even smell the dusty sweetness of the house where we were going to live.

I felt, as Emily looked into my eyes, that she could see how hard it had been, the past three weeks of trying to make a life for my children in this place where we were on our own and lost. I could see her feeling compassion and deciding to take us in. Emily and I were not exactly strangers any more after that moment, although we didn't know each other yet. The boys and I moved in the next morning.

Aiden, Tris and I shared a large bedroom in the back of the house, right next to the bathroom and, just beyond that, the kitchen. It had been Emily's room but she had shifted into a smaller one off the veranda on the east side of the house. Our room looked out on the back garden and was sunny and breezy, with windows along two walls. There was a big bed for the boys to share and a little bed for me.

The doors of Emily's house were painted a lovely shade of violet and hung with lace curtains. On the walls were old pictures of Emily's long-ago family—Victorian Māori ladies with high-piled hair and elaborate pearl jewelry. All through the house there were windows of glass slats, which were always open to let the breeze blow through and keep the house cool. The ceiling—the underside of the tin roof —was very high, and when it rained it sounded like thunder. A wide veranda in front and down one side of the house was filled with dilapidated chairs and tables, and ferns growing in elderly tea kettles. From the backyard we could see a mountain, Iku-rangi, "The Tail of the Sky".

"We have God here," Emily said, and it seemed to me she was right.

In addition to God, we seemingly also had ghosts. Emily told me not to worry. "They only bother the bad people, not good people like you," she said. This did not have the completely comforting effect she intended.

The ghosts, who were maybe ancestors, chased away tenants who were bad for Emily. They had chased away a hippie girl who did something with a Mormon missionary that Emily wouldn't discuss much. "Oh, the thing I saw," she said. "It was disgusting. Right on the veranda." I tried not to look like the sort of person who would ever do anything disgusting on a veranda. (I also tried to look like the sort of person who wouldn't mind hearing a bit more about it.)

Emily's late husband, Frank, was a white man from New Zealand who hadn't believed in ghosts. "Frank told me, 'If you want to see a ghost badly enough, you will'," Emily said. However, despite his lack of sympathy he had moved their young daughter, Emona, out of a bedroom in the house that contained an old wardrobe after Emona told Emily and Frank that a man came out of the mirror every night to play with her in the dark. After Frank moved her into a different bedroom she never saw the man again.

The wardrobe was still in a corner of the disused room, slowly being eaten into dust by generations of insects. Its faded mirror reflected the four-poster bed that no one ever slept in now.

As well as the ghosts, there were two Mormon missionaries living in Emily's house. Their bedroom was at the front of the house, but they had their own bath and a kitchen of sorts on the veranda so at first we didn't see them much. Like the ghosts, they were choosy.

Wednesday, August 28
Kia orana everyone,
        After many mishaps, some more amusing than

others, and much use of my newly discovered patience,
I am finally: (one) settled in a house, (two) driving
around in a car and (three) doing the research with
artists that I came to do.

The house belongs to an elderly widow named
Emily, who lost her much beloved husband, Frank, ten
years ago. For the time being we also share the house
with two Mormon missionaries from America, Elder
Smith (the elder Elder at twenty) and Elder Winston
(the younger Elder, who is only nineteen). They are
fine, upstanding young men who seem to have got over
their initial shock at suddenly finding themselves living
with the boys and me. (If I had known it was going to
rain while we were out the first day and that Emily
would rescue our laundry off the line and festoon it
gaily around the kitchen, I would have held off washing
some of my more entertaining underclothes.)

It is a beautiful, rambling house with wide
verandas and high ceilings. Emily has lived in it, she
says, "from the cradle". Emily is eighty-two.

The car is a rental, minuscule and somewhat
expensive. I almost bought a car—a battered refugee
from a Polynesian demolition derby. "It'll be fine as
long as you don't drive it too far," the man at the car
place said. There are less than fifty miles of road,
paved and unpaved, in the whole country. It is less
than ten miles by road between any two points on the

island. "Oh, I'm just going to the grocery store and things like that," I assured him. "How far do you live from the grocery store?" he asked, looking concerned. That's when I became suspicious.

For the equivalent of about eight dollars anyone can get a Cook Islands driver's licence. There's no test—it's just to make some fast cash off the tourists, who get them as souvenirs, mostly never intending to actually drive. Just in case, though, there's a big poster on the wall of the police station that says: "We Drive on the LEFT Side of the Road". I proudly produced my still warm licence at the car rental agency. "Hard to get one o' them, eh?" winked the Kiwi boy behind the counter. "We drive on the left side of the road," he said as I headed out the door. (This was quite unnecessary. As anyone who has driven with me in the US will attest, I frequently drive on the left.)

There are no traffic lights or stop signs on Rarotonga. There is, however, a traffic circle in downtown Avarua right by the Seven Coconut Trees —which are touted by our guidebook as a tourist attraction. Surrounded as they are by approximately seventy thousand other coconut trees, the appeal of these seven trees to tourists seems to be quite minimal. Anyway, it's funny how simple things can quite suddenly seem very complicated when you try to do them backwards and upside-down at forty kilometres per hour. Our first trip through the traffic circle—well, I wouldn't necessarily use the word "harrowing". Let's just say the wild chickens aren't quite as sure of themselves as they used to be. Tris has been avenged.

While we were at the beach the other day a man caught an octopus. It was still alive when he brought it to shore, writhing and undulating. The boys and I went over to see. The octopus was three feet across and feisty.

"You can touch it if you want," the man offered, as a stray tentacle snaked its way up his calf. We took a step back in unison.

"That's okay," I squeaked. "We'll just watch."

I sat a few yards down the sand thinking about other things while the man bashed the octopus senseless on a rock. Behind me, the volcano rose up out of the jungle; in front of me, the Pacific Ocean stretched away with no other landfall until Antarctica. After a while, Aiden came strolling up with a clam shell as big as a soup bowl; he was using it as a sand shovel. "I'm worried about you, Mom," he said, very seriously. "You seem to have lost your sense of adventure."

Kia manuia, everyone. Don't let the tentacles get you.

Love, Kathy

In the mornings Emily went to mass at the Catholic church down the road, just on the edge of town. My desire to appear to be a good Catholic mother did not extend to the extreme of attending dawn mass, so from seven o'clock until eight o'clock we had the house to ourselves and I revelled in the brief semi-solitude. I was shy about sharing Emily's house with her—especially those morning moments when you are vulnerable and naked, before you have your public face on for the day. Even fully dressed people are naked before eight a.m. Left to my own devices I would have lurked around in my bedroom, a phantom of those interstitial times, but unfortunately I had managed to raise Aiden and Tris without their having a similar desire for invisibility, and after three weeks of being trapped in hotel rooms they damn sure weren't going to sit on their bed. Emily's yard had trees to climb and space to run in, and there were big rocks on the shore next to the ocean. And there was Emily herself, who would talk to you, or show you how to get a pawpaw down from a high tree by using a special forked stick. And because Aiden and Tris were irrepressibly *out* in this house, I was, reluctantly, too. And so I began, very slowly and awkwardly, to know Emily.

Emily occasionally made silk-screened clothes—shirts and sarongs, or pareu—with pictures of tiare māori, the wild gardenia that blooms everywhere on the island, Tangaroa, god of the sea and fertility, or a village of thatched huts under palm trees. She had a workroom with an ancient sewing machine, beautiful if dilapidated screens stacked against the walls, and sample shirts hanging here and there on bent wire hangers. However, she seemed to have no customers, and no particular interest in attracting them.

She told me it had been Frank's idea to start silk-screening. They had sold the shirts to homesick Cook Islanders living in New Zealand. "They used to cry so," she said. "They would cry over missing the tiare." Frank would design and make the screens, they would both do the printing on fabric, and Emily would sew up the finished shirts. I wanted to ask her to make some for us, but felt too shy.

It was around this time that Elise came to take me to a gallery opening, which would be my first foray into the Rarotongan art world and the real start of my research. Given how afraid I was to talk to Emily, you may be surprised that what I do for a living is talk to people. Either I talk to people about their lives, or I talk to classes about what these people have told me. I'll admit this does seem an odd career for me, but when I'm talking to people as part of my work they are telling me about themselves: I am not telling them about me.

I have always been reluctant to tell anyone about myself because I think—well, strongly suspect—I may be odd, and not in a charming, offbeat kind of way but in the socio-emotional equivalent of having accidentally tucked the hem of your skirt into the back waistband of your pantyhose. That kind of odd. And the problem with knowing someone is that, once you start to build a relationship, he or she will pretty quickly pick up on your oddness.

As far as people on the island were concerned, then, the important thing for me was not to build real relationships with them. I didn't plan to *know* anyone, and I certainly didn't plan for anyone to know me. It is completely possible that every white person who has ever been to live in the South Seas has been driven by the same feeling of oddness and the need to get far away from other people, those excruciating witnesses of our damaged and defeated lives. This is a large part of the allure of vast stretches of ocean and sparsely scattered populations. Read a biography of Paul Gauguin some time: there was a man with a skirt tucked into his socio-emotional pantyhose, for sure.

In the event, I steeled myself and went to the opening, taking the boys with me. The gallery was run by a woman named Kay George. I met a sculptor called Ted, who someone told me was in line to be the next high chief, or ariki, of the island. He introduced me to one of his friends, a painter called Tim Buchanan. And I met a man named Nate Flynn, another painter. He thought it was nice I had brought the boys along with me. "Good on you," he said twice. After we had looked at the art, the boys ran around outside while I stood on the front porch of the gallery and chatted to Ted and Tim and Nate and Kay, asking them about themselves, telling them nothing about me. We had to leave early though, because Aiden got too close to the hot exhaust pipe of one of the motorbikes parked in front and burned his calf. "That's what we call a Rarotonga tattoo," Nate said to him. The next morning there was a red patch on Aiden's leg that was exactly the same squashed-circle shape as the island.

The afternoon had made me realise, though, that I wouldn't be able to take the boys everywhere with me. If I wanted to be able to talk to people about themselves without little boys interjecting every few minutes, the boys would have to be elsewhere. For every other moment of our time we would be together, but for the interviews we would have to be apart.

Emily introduced me to Mata, who took care of her garden. "She is my angel from the Lord," Emily said. Mata had a grown-up daughter in New Zealand, but also seemed to have semi-adopted a girl named Kali, who was just Aiden's age. Mata would watch Aiden and Tris for me for four hours on Monday afternoons so I could work on my research. It took me a while to figure out that this was the plan, mostly because I couldn't understand a word Mata said. She had a quavering, cracked voice that reminded me of the aging Katharine Hepburn in *The Lion In Winter*, when she says of her jewelled necklace: "I would hang it from my nipples, only it would shock the children." Whatever Mata was saying ended on an interrogative note. I smiled and gingerly agreed. Mata looked at me as though I were a little slow-witted and in need of being treated with gentle kindness.

The first day of the new arrangement, Mata said something to me and I smiled my idiot smile of assent. It seemed they were going to feed her pigs. She lifted Aiden and Tris into the back of her battered pickup truck and the three of them went screaming off down the road, the boys shrieking with delight. My heart leapt to my throat, cutting off most of my ability to breathe and all of my ability to think about research. Six hours later they arrived back late—Mata didn't have a watch—with ice-cream cones and Kali. I had been wracked with longing for them and had to restrain myself from engulfing them with relief. They were sticky and wind-blown and happy. Mata had named two of her pigs after them.

The Christian missionaries who set off for the South Seas believed that industrial nineteenth-century London, with its filth, fetid air and Malthusian brutality, was the world as God intended it after the loss of Eden. They took seriously the lines in Genesis where humanity was condemned because of the sin of Adam and Eve, and God told Adam, "Cursed is the ground for thy sake; thorns also and thistles shall it bring forth for thee; In the sweat of thy face shalt thou eat bread, 'til thou return unto the ground; for out of it wast thou taken: for dust thou art, and unto dust shalt thou return."

It was a vengeful curse from a vengeful god, but when the missionaries sailed into the bay at Tahiti and stepped on to the shores of an island that was so fertile bread-like fruit was falling from the trees, they found the biggest problem people faced with regard to food was not getting brained by it. Could it be that the long-ago garden still existed in these faraway islands? The idea was theologically problematic, and more than a few missionaries ended up forsaking the God of vengeance for the angels of Eden, with their swaying hips and baskets of fruit.

At Emily's house, pawpaws were falling off the trees faster than we could eat them, and bananas were massing in huge bunches in a grove out the back of the garden. I was devouring at least two pawpaws a day and Emily was bringing in more every morning, urging us to eat them before they went bad. They tasted like lovely summer flowers. The boys didn't particularly like them, but Tris put a big dent in the bananas before he burned out.

We were also overloaded with tomatoes, oranges, sweet potatoes and watercress, but the pawpaws were the biggest problem. Every Monday, Mata took the rotten ones from the past week to feed to the pigs she was raising on a patch of land in Avatiu, just inland. She was always intending to eat the pigs when they got big, but she would give them names and look after them, seeing they were well and happy, and inevitably fall in love with them. After all that, of course, she couldn't stand to kill them. As a consequence, she was starting to have a lot of pigs.

Mata took the boys with her every Monday to feed the pigs. Sometimes I would pass them on the road, me going one way and they going the other. Aiden, Tris and sometimes Kali would be standing up on the bed of Mata's red pickup truck, looking out over the cab or sideways over the truck bed to wave excitedly at me. "Sit down! Sit *down!*" I would yell out my window and they would momentarily sit down, but when I looked back they would be standing up again. Alvis used to say that in Guatemala there was a big black dog that came out at night and followed drunks and little children home, to keep them safe and guard them from harm. There were wild dogs all over Rarotonga and Alvis must have been right, because no matter what Aiden and Tris did that I would never have let them do in the United States, they never got so much as a scratch.

Journal
Thursday, September 5
   Wake-up time for me this morning: not quite dawn and Aiden is out of bed, wants to go to the

bathroom, but is afraid someone will see him in his boxer shorts and T-shirt so he wants me to check the coast is clear. Then I take a shower and can hear the boys singing at the tops of their lungs in the bedroom.

I come out and dress, and then start pumping water through our water purifier so we have clean water to drink. (Boiling it also works, but the worms that float down from the reservoir are unappetising even after they have been boiled.)

Tris wants to watch. Tris wants me to get him a chair to stand on so he can see better. Tris wants to help. Tris says he's cold—he wants to get dressed. Tris is hungry—he wants to pour the cereal himself. Aiden says he thinks he has a fever. I feel his forehead and it's warm. I quickly finish pumping water. We have about seven litres. It has taken me half an hour to get them. I give both Tris and Aiden some decongestant. I give Tris some cereal with milk. Aiden feels too bad to get up and get dressed. He is in my bed. Tris is spitting chewed cereal on to the tablecloth. I make myself a cup of coffee and clean up Tris's mess. Emily comes home from dawn Mass and talks to me. Tris says he is still hungry and wants toast and juice. Not that juice, the other juice. Aiden is calling from the bedroom,"Mom Mom Mom Mom Mom Mom Mom Mom Mom Mom." He wants a hug and help putting on his shorts so he can come out. He is hungry. He doesn't want any breakfast. Tris needs his nose wiped. He wants to butter his own toast. I make the beds. Emily is still talking to me. So is Aiden. So is Tris. None of them are talking about the same thing. They all talk at once.

A man named Peter comes in to bring Emily vegetables. Emily says Peter is her angel from the Lord, which is also what she calls Mata. Peter is nice. I drink my coffee and do the dishes. The boys are wrestling in the bedroom. Aiden says he is cold. I have to help him put on his socks and shoes. I check carefully for spiders because a big one has been running around in our wardrobe for the past few days. Tris has wiped snot all over the front of his shirt. By now it is 8.30—I have been up two hours. The boys and I are all dressed and Tris, at least, has had breakfast.

I put the boys into the car and we go into town. I drop off film for Elder Smith at the photo store and then go to the CITC looking for supplies for Aiden to do magic tricks—he still feels bad. I buy two bags of balloons, a newspaper and the only cassette tape they have, then we drive to the store to try and buy string. We end up with thread, which is as close as we can get. Aiden is feeling terrible. We drive around the island until ten o'clock when the pictures are ready, listening to the cassette tape "Human Clay" by Creed— and running the air-conditioner.

We come home and I give Elder Smith his pictures and Emily the newspaper. Tris disappears with his balloons. I have to carry Aiden inside to bed. I give him some Tylenol. Tris reappears and wants some too. Aiden wants water, warm—not cold. Tris wants me to blow up his balloons. Tris is pestering Aiden. Aiden wants to go out to the porch. Tris has so much snot on his shirt that it needs to be changed. Aiden is hungry; Tris is hungry. Aiden wants to run around the house to let off steam. Tris spills a litre of water all over himself and the floor of our room. I clean it up and change his pants and start boiling the water for pasta for lunch. Aiden comes in and sits down. Tris comes in and they start to play a game where they push each other off chairs. I send them both to the porch. Now it's 11.30—I begin making lunch and they push each other off the chairs on the porch. I'm starting to sneeze.

Last night in bed before I put out the light, I watched four moko hunting moths on the ceiling over my head. After the light was off, I heard them bark at each other, and then there was a squishy splat on the floor next to my bed. It hadn't occurred to me that moko could fall off ceilings. I have decided to sleep with the sheets over my head, no matter how hot it gets.

When I was young my little brother Joe and I spent two weeks in Jakarta as tourists. We arrived in the middle of a cholera epidemic and the city—not the tidiest of places in the best of times—was like a war zone. There were flooded sewers and rubble and rats. I have a memory, which *must* be wrong, of seeing a corpse in a street. And I remember, after a long grim trek in sweltering afternoon heat in search of something we never found, suddenly coming upon a gleaming, perfect, pink and orange Dunkin' Donuts—just plopped down there, like the part in *The Wizard Of Oz* where Judy Garland opens the door of Aunty Em's black-and-white Kansas farmhouse and finds the Technicolor Munchkin Land in the front yard. After two weeks of even having to brush my teeth in antibacterial, prophylactic gin, Dunkin' Donuts seemed like a dream come true. It was cool inside, and clean. It was also empty. Two smiling young Indonesian women stood behind glass display cases that showed, in their spotless sterility, that not only were there no donuts now, but there had never been any donuts.

As it happened I didn't care about the donuts: I had my eyes firmly fixed on a juice machine behind the counter. It was one of those movie-theatre juice machines. On top were two clear, aquarium-sized boxes, each displaying a continuously circling fountain of coloured juice, one pink, one orange. The juice squirted on to the ceiling of the box and then ran down the sides in a waterfall of cooling lusciousness. Outside, the air was a hundred degrees, with one hundred percent humidity. Juice.

In a combination of pidgin English and pantomime, the young women gave us the bad news: there was no juice. When the Dunkin' Donuts shop had arrived—deposited by helicopter, pre-fabricated and already stocked with pink and orange squirty juice—the Operations Instruction booklet dropped down by the departing pilot was only in English, and incomprehensible at that. No one had been able to figure out how to get the juice to come out of the machine, or how to make anything else work, for that matter. The same juice had been rotating in the boxes for over a year, while Dunkin' Donuts executives at their head office in Canton, Massachusetts lamented the lack of sales in the Indonesian division but kept sending the pay cheques anyway.

The Cook Islands Post Office bore some striking similarities to the Jakarta branch of Dunkin' Donuts in that nothing functioned quite as promised. My guidebook had a section headed "Post and Communications". "You can receive mail care of Poste Restante at the post office," it confidently asserted, "where it is held for thirty days. To collect mail at the post office in Avarua, it should be addressed to you c/o Poste Restante, Avarua, Rarotonga, Cook Islands. Poste Restante services are available on the other islands."

After more than a month I had not received a scrap of

mail, despite both my father and a friend called Jonathan having assured me by email that they had written. My father had sent two boxes of desperately needed books for my research. Jonathan had sent only love.

Jonathan was my oldest friend. I had liked him from the time I met him during the first week of our freshman year at college. It took me a few years, though, before I knew I loved him. One night in his dorm room, after weeks of tortuous flirtation, we finally kissed. We lived together for a year after that. Then he went to graduate school in Chicago and I went to North Carolina. We held on for a while, until I called him in Chicago to tell him I wanted to break up. He cried on the phone. I felt wretched. "Poor Jonathan," I thought, "this must be terrible for him."

A few weeks later I called his apartment to check on him—at least that's what I told myself. I wanted to make sure he was recovering, however slowly. He didn't answer the phone. Perhaps, I flattered myself, the recovery wasn't going so well. A few days later I tried again. No answer. Again and again and again—all hours of the day and night. For days and days this went on. "Oh, god," I thought, "maybe he's killed himself. He's lying dead and unmissed on the floor of his apartment. Why, why, did I have to break his poor, tender heart?" I feared my rejection was too much for him to ever recover from.

Finally, I got a phone company recording on the line.

"The number you are calling," it said, "has been changed." I called the new number. A woman answered. "Is Jonathan there?" I asked, taken aback. "Darling," I heard her say, "it's for you." He had recovered.

We had not spoken for fifteen years after that when, out of the blue, about a year before I left for Rarotonga, he emailed me. We had resumed our old friendship but on a purely platonic basis, and when I got to the island I missed hearing from him every couple of days. I lay in my narrow bed and stared into the dark, wondering what he was doing, remembering how it was to be with him long ago, and thinking how good it was to be friends with him again, how it felt like coming home. I wrote letters, more than I ever thought I would. He was living on the other side of the world in Switzerland, on the last dregs of his marriage to the woman who had answered the phone. Their relationship hadn't turned out well in the end.

About two weeks after we moved in, Emily got up in the middle of the night to go to the bathroom, but fell in the darkness and hurt her back. "Didn't you hear me?" she said, but I hadn't. All I heard at night now was the surf and the moko barking on the ceiling. I had even stopped hearing the Air New Zealand flight that arrived and departed between two and three in the morning on Tuesdays and Saturdays. This was the plane that had brought us to the island, and the only plane if you didn't count the Air Rarotonga mosquito that flew between the island and another island, Aitutaki, a couple of times a day.

The first time the Air New Zealand jet had flown over our roof on its way in to land, I thought it was crashing into our house. I thought as it came nearer and nearer and nearer that I would have to scream. I thought we would all die. Soon, though, I was sleeping through it; the plane had nothing more to do with us.

Now I had also slept through the sound of Emily falling over. After this, she was not entirely bedridden, although I think she would like to have been. She stopped going to Mass at dawn every morning. Handsome Father Kevin usually said Mass so I knew Emily must be in bad shape, but I could still see her out the window, stooping to pick flowers for 'eis—the Rarotongan leis she made for the Castaway Beach Villas. She crouched painfully under the frangipani tree, slowly gathering fallen blossoms into a plastic bag from the CITC while the elders sat on the veranda twenty feet from her, reading their Bibles and the Book of Mormon.

"Rain" is Somerset Maugham's famous story of a missionary's fall from grace with an American prostitute named Sadie Thompson, while the two of them are stranded together in the interminable rain of Pago Pago in Samoa. As I had been raised in America witnessing outrageous depravity on the part of the morally self-righteous, the story's final twist never had a chance of surprising me: "missionary" plus "prostitute" plus "rain" equalled pretty much a foregone conclusion.

Imagine how intriguing it was, then, when I found myself living for a time with two actual missionaries, those strange and disturbing beings. By accident I spilled pickle juice all over Elder Winston's pants one day and then offered to wash them for him, and mend them where the hem had come undone. This was, as God is my witness, completely unpremeditated. If I *had* been premeditating getting Elder Winston out of his pants, and it was ridiculously easy, I would not have chosen to do it in full view of both children, Emily, Mata, and the man who had come to read the electric meter. In any case, I avoided both the missionaries after that and was relieved when they moved out. "Rain", after all, is not a happy story. In one way, though, the elders—a funny title for two such hopelessly young boys—were especially useful. From the moment Elder Winston stepped out on to the veranda wearing only his white shirt, black plastic name tag, and a towel, holding his pants in his hand, I pretty much stopped thinking about Gregg naked.

Also, they were awfully nice to Aiden and Tris.

Now, though, I wanted to slap them. Instead, I hustled the boys through their cornflakes and we headed out with plastic bags to the bit of blossom-strewn lawn most conspicuous to our pious housemates. As we picked flowers I ranted in my head, spitting words back and forth across my brain, but as we worked our way around to the side of the house where guava trees grew alongside the frangipani trees I forgot the elders, because Aiden picked up the fallen flowers so carefully. "Is this a good one?" he asked me each time, holding the pale bloom up to me before he put it in his bag. He and Tris looked luminous and tender in the dappled early morning shade. Tris seemed to have a pearly glow. His eyes were starting to change color, I noticed. They used to be brown; now they were becoming green.

We finally headed to the very end of the garden, down by the beach, scattering the hens and their chicks. We couldn't see the house at all from there, only the beach and the sea and the road along the coast. As we picked tiare māori, the wild gardenias, their scent was heady on the ocean breeze, almost too strong to be beautiful. I could smell the water too—salt, seaweed, and ten thousand miles of emptiness. The day was still cool.

When we got back to the house, the elders had disappeared. Gone to do God's work, I supposed. I gave Emily the bags. It takes fifty tiare and thirty tipani to make one 'ei.

"There are 367 tiare," I told her, "and 192 tipani."

"Just like Frank." She smiled at me. "He used to count the flowers, too."

I had done it without noticing what I was doing. My

back was tired from bending over. I hadn't realised how much stooped labour was involved in being a woman in the third world.

Later I sat on the floor in Emily's bedroom and sewed the 'eis on a string of raffia. Emily was in bed and her friend Dolly had come to visit, bringing pawpaws and oranges. Other people brought us tomatoes, starfruit, more oranges and a big bunch of bananas. Emily rested in bed and she and Dolly talked above my head while I was working, the flowers and leaves spread out on a towel on the floor in front of me. Tris came in to be with me, bobbing around like a tipsy cork on rough seas, and then went out again to climb the frangipani trees in the garden. We had an order for four 'eis; I put the rest of the flowers in the refrigerator to keep them fresh until the next plane came in. We made $1.50 for each 'ei. Emily split the money with me fifty:fifty. Then she gave the boys a dollar each from her share.

Although sometimes trouble is just plain trouble, it can also happen that sometimes trouble holds a secret benediction. How else, after all, do you come to love someone so much that they are a part of you? It was in those days when we first moved into her house and when she was so hurt from her fall, that we came to be Emily's family and she came to be ours.

To imagine it the way it was, you have to see her room with one door open to the workroom and all the lovely silk-screens leaning against the walls and one door open to the veranda with the sun warming a golden square of floor. You have to imagine me barefoot in the early morning kitchen, making tea and slicing bread for toast with the radio on low, and ukulele music coming out of it to mingle with the sounds of roosters crowing and Tris's breathless baby voice prattling to Emily in her bed, while she tells him legends and fairy tales from the island, the stories her mother and her grandmother told her. You have to imagine Emily showing Aiden how to string the tiare blossoms on a long strand of raffia, and Aiden being serious and careful with the big silver needle, concentrating hard while Emily watches over him and I sit on the floor next to them with hundreds of flowers in heaps on a big, worn bath towel, keeping count inside my head—ten tiare, four leaves, six tipani (the local word for frangipani), four leaves, ten tiare, four leaves, six tipani—while I make the 'eis for the Castaway and listen to them talk.

You have to see Emily and me in the heat of the afternoon, sitting in the shade of the veranda while Aiden and Tris clamber in the branches of the tipani tree, up among the flowers, and Emily tells me stories from her life. You have to see us when no one else is around, or when Mata comes, bringing the mail from Emily's post office box, and Emily reads aloud parts of a letter from Elizabeth while Mata eats a piece of banana cake that Emily made in the morning. You have to see Tris fall asleep on a settee on the veranda and then wake up an hour later to find us all still there exactly as we were. You have to imagine that we can always hear the sound of the ocean, and that there is always breeze enough to stir the air inside the house. You have to imagine a world where it is always an afternoon in summer.

The Mormon missionaries left; the Mission House renovations were finally finished and the head missionary came with a white van and took all their stuff away. They followed with their bikes, dragging their trash can up the driveway between them on their way out. The boys and I moved into their bedroom out on the front veranda, facing the ocean and the rocky beach at the end of the garden. Emily's second daughter, Emona, would have our room soon, when she came for a visit.

Emily seemed quite happy to have the elders gone, although they "hadn't been so bad". It was just us in the house now. At night I would sit on the front steps, listening to the quiet house and the strange rattling sound of the palms.

Emily regretted that she had sold her old piano. She gave piano lessons on it for years and years. She said that she would have taught Aiden to play. "I have my own method," she said, and the way she said it suddenly made me see a barefoot little kid sitting next to Emily in the airy workroom, bent over the keys in the soft light and the stillness that is made up of all the sounds of the surf and the palm trees and the birds.

"And—oh!—the parties we would have!" Emily said. She had gone back to the days when Frank was still alive, and I could tell by the look in her eyes as she glanced around the veranda that she was seeing it peopled with friends and family who weren't there any more. I could tell she was hearing Frank's voice. "I would be at the piano, going like the wind!" she said. "How we would sing! Everyone had a good time. We would have our gin and tonic but everyone was so nice, not like these things now, drunken and fighting …" Her voice trailed off. "If only these walls could tell the stories," she said, and she was back again.

She told me about a party that had taken place when Elizabeth, her daughter from her first marriage, was a little girl. To keep Elizabeth and her cousin out of trouble her mother had given them a coconut each and told them to plant them. "Those two trees grew from the coconuts," she said, and I looked up at two coconut palms right next to each other in the garden, swaying high above us. They were old trees now but in the shade of them Elizabeth was always still a little girl, even though it had been more than half a century ago.

When Elizabeth was a little older, at one of the parties there was a Mormon missionary who kept flirting with her. He had been slowly falling in love with Elizabeth, who was very beautiful, and he was beginning to press his case.

"Elizabeth climbed right up that coconut tree where he couldn't follow her," Emily laughed. "She sat up there for the whole evening and wouldn't come down. She said, 'No, no, no! I won't marry you!'"

Not too long after that, Elizabeth had taken orders and become a Catholic nun. Now she was a Mother Superior living in New Zealand. Emily missed her very much.

The Cook Islands Democratic Party had also started on the veranda. When Emily's cousin, Tom Davis, was running for prime minister in 1978, Emily and Frank's house had been the organising centre for his campaign. He had won and become the Cook Islands' second prime minister after independence. He and his party held office until 1987. "If these walls could tell the stories," Emily said again, only she was sadder now.

While we were on the island, Aiden and Tris didn't go to school. Tris was only three, but Aiden was seven and missing second grade. Frankly, I thought, there's time enough to learn all the state capitals when you're dead.

To compensate, I tried to channel the scientific verve traditional of Westerners in the South Seas. We flushed the toilet and carefully noted the direction of the resulting whirlpool (clockwise). Unfortunately I had neglected to

remember the direction of spin back in Colorado, so as
a scientific investigation it didn't exactly rank with anything from Captain Cook and Joseph Banks, but on the
bright side at least we hadn't decimated any indigenous
populations with syphilis, Christianity and rats. I tried to
compensate for the toilet disappointment by bringing the
boys out into the garden at night to lie on our backs and
try to find the Southern Cross. It was harder to find than
I thought it would be, hidden in vast oceans of firework
stars scattered so thickly across the night that they lit up
even a moonless sky. We would lie on the ground until
vertigo grabbed us and we felt ourselves falling out into
the far reaches of space.

The experience reminded me of how Halley's Comet
had come when Jonathan and I were in college. We had
been told that we would have to escape the lights of
Boston in order to see it, so one weekend we drove far
north, through the woods and all the way to a small
peninsula on the Maine coast. We arrived just at sundown
and watched the moon and the sun set almost together,
the moon a sliver of gold leaning into the bloody sky,
while we sat in the car kissing and getting colder and
colder waiting for darkness.

Finally, when the night was black enough, we discovered we couldn't find the comet. Against the dazzling,
wheeling mosaic of stars, we couldn't orient ourselves
to the meagre little star chart we'd clipped from Sunday's

Boston Globe. We couldn't even find the North Star in all that wild profusion of the heavens. We ended up standing in a snowy field kissing some more, and then sleeping warm and close together in a cheap motel on Route 1. When I got back to Boston, I called my grandmother in Arkansas and she said, "Well shoot, I see it every night right here from the backyard. It's not much."

I stopped by the post office once a week to see if there was any mail for me but there never was. The two nice kids who worked there started to feel sorry for me. At first they would diligently search through the Poste Restante box, but as time wore on they would just glance up when I came in, give me a doleful look and slowly shake their heads. Then, after almost two months, I got two letters that my father had mailed from Arkansas the first week of August, and one from Jonathan in Switzerland. The kids were happy—or maybe just relieved.

Now that we were not in the hotel I didn't have regular computer access any more. There were four mostly working computers in the post office, which I tried to use to send emails. When I checked for the non-existent letters from my non-existent friends, I used one of the computers to send my father a quick email saying that we were okay. I had to make it quick because the computer chairs had wheels on them and Tris and Aiden were using them to race each other across the room, squealing with delight and crashing madly into the tourists waiting in line to buy postcard stamps.

Emily's back got worse instead of better, and twice we took her in the car up the side of the mountain to the hospital and waited while she got X-rayed. All they could tell us was that nothing was broken. At first she was getting out of bed for most of the day, but that gradually happened less and less. Most days, Mata came by for a while to help take care of her, but often she and I and the boys were alone together. Her friends dropped by to see her sometimes and she received them in bed. I would make tea for them and bring it in on a tray with fruit and biscuits—like the daughter of the house would do. In the mornings, I made Emily the breakfast she liked—soft-boiled eggs, grilled tomatoes and toast.

In the afternoons we moved out to the veranda, where it was cooler. I was beginning to teach Tris his letters and he would sit in my lap singing the ABC song. Aiden was reading his way through all the children's books in the library and when we went there we always brought Emily back a book. Johnny, the librarian, kept an eye out and saved things she thought Emily might like, usually books about the island.

I took Emily's list of errands with us into town and one day Johnny saw me checking it off. "I see Emily's made you into one of the family," she said, laughing. "Welcome to Polynesia."

In the middle of September Tris turned four. I bought a chocolate cake from the Turoa Bakery, made butter-cream frosting, and decorated the cake with toy racing cars from the Bounty Bookshop. Kali, Mata and Emily came to the party in the kitchen. Aiden gave Tris pick-up sticks, I gave him a toy car transporter with two jeeps, and Kali gave him a book and a balloon-animal maker. After a while we went to Just Burgers, which had a sign outside proclaiming "America-Style Burgers": they featured such American-style toppings as fried egg, spinach and cucumber. We loved the burgers, but I started to wonder if I should give Just Burgers some French-fry advice, such as that they are supposed to be *fried*, not just left out in the sun to defrost.

In late September, Emily's daughter Emona arrived with her husband and two children. We had now been living with Emily for more than a month and in the crucible of her back injury had begun to make a little family, so it was strange having her *real* family around. Emily and I would blush guiltily when Emona came across us sitting together talking on the veranda. Feeling we were too familiar, I reluctantly withdrew with the boys back into our own room and kitchen and bathroom. These rooms had once been my preferred lair, but now they seemed too shut off from the world—our world. I took the boys for long rides in the car around and around the circle of the island, feeling exiled. Emily stopped me on the veranda one afternoon as we were heading in. She put her hand gently on my arm and said, "I told Emona that I think she has chased away my friend." I smiled and disagreed and made an excuse, but Emily was right. And I missed her.

Aiden woke up one day with the side of his neck swollen like an orange. The doctor in town—not Dr Kush, who we heard had gone north in pursuit of her errant husband, but Dr Tamarua, who had a jaunty auburn toupée—diagnosed mumps. It seemed possible, although Aiden had been immunised against mumps before we left the States. Undeterred, the doctor prescribed a course of antibiotics. Was there a particular type I preferred? What did I think the dosage should be? I am rather unclear about these things myself, but I leapt into the breach with Zithromax, the only antibiotic whose name I could remember. "What the hell," I thought to myself. "Now is not the time to lose courage."

Emona and her family left for three days in Aitutaki and it was just us again. Emily and I went back to spending our mornings sitting on the veranda while the boys rambled around us like giant butterflies. We had an order for eighty-two 'eis for the following Saturday, when a big feast was planned for the Castaway, so we started work right away, keeping the finished garlands in the refrigerator to the exclusion of actual food. Soon, though, we were running very thin on flowers. Mata made a secret midnight raid on someone's "sleepy hibiscus" bushes and I drove down to the CITC, boldly denuded the bougainvillea bushes, and fled in the car.

One Sunday night we went to the Mormons' "Musical Fireside". Elder Smith and Elder Winston had come by to invite us specially: they were trying to convert us now they no longer lived with us. At the Fireside each had a wild gardenia bud behind one ear; they looked rather too smooth and charming. Nga was there. We hadn't seen her in a while—not since we moved out of the motel. We sat next to her and Tris fell asleep in her lap. We didn't get converted though.

In the long quiet afternoons at home, sometimes I would sing slow songs from my childhood to the boys— "Danny Boy" and "Shenandoah". One afternoon Aiden wanted something peppier so I sang him "Froggie Went A-Courtin'", but Tris, sprawled languorously across me, objected to the raucous rollicking. He liked the sad ones. "Sing the midnight songs," he said.

I have a picture of Aiden and Tris from those days. They are asleep in bed, curled on their sides facing each other. In their sleep, they are holding hands.

Once we moved in with Emily and I finally stopped shushing them, they didn't need to be shushed anymore. Once I stopped trying to make them always behave well, they behaved beautifully. Once I stopped trying to mould them into wonderful children, they transcended every parenting plan and every ideal about childhood and every magazine article about how to raise perfect children and became, instead of perfect children, lovely children, vibrant and alive, smelling of earth and rain, warm in the sunlight, tender and bright and beautiful. It was like living with a pair of lion cubs. Or young bears. Or fallen angels.

Wednesday, September 25

    Elder Smith and Elder Winston came by to visit us today. They brought candy for the boys. They asked me if I had any religious questions for them. I suddenly felt the ghost of Sadie Thompson laughing from the eaves. With great self-restraint, I declined to have any religious questions.

RAIN

Emona and her family stayed a couple of weeks and then early in October, just as the rainy season was starting, they packed up and took Emily with them to spend three months in New Zealand. Emily would be dividing her time between Emona's house and Elizabeth's convent. She seemed to have no qualms about going off for so long and leaving me in her house, watched over only by the ghosts. In one fell swoop, I had found everything I longed for. I was alone with my two magical boys, living in a dreamlike house in the middle of a wild gorgeous garden, warm at last after the long cold winter, on an island all my own.

There is a sour note left over from our Puritan heritage that says, "Be careful what you wish for." It's a lie: our wishes are just as likely to make us happy as they are to make us sad. In some ways I had wished for outrageous things—a tropical paradise and a year to do whatever I wanted there—but in another way I had wished only for nothing—nothing to do and nowhere to go, no trials, no successes, no failures, no possessions, no friends, no enemies, no lovers, no alarm clocks, no appointment books, no deadlines.

The world has a way, though, of being so much more than you can ever imagine. As the Mad Hatter told Alice, it's very easy to have more than nothing. I got almost nothing to do and my happy boys to do it with, no possessions and a passionfruit vine heavy with fruit growing in the backyard, no alarm clocks and a sky of heartbreaking lapis blue and rains like God's own fury, no success and the heavy warmth of my child's hand in my own.

And so, having got every nothing I had wished for and more, I now sank into our life as though I were sinking into a warm bath—or into the warm buoyant water of the lagoon, or the perfumed bed of tipani blossoms carpeting the springtime grass of our garden.

The very *wet* grass of our garden. It began raining steadily around the clock two days before Emily left. It came down hard, like a fat man falling into bed. Rain has a bad reputation. Somerset Maugham made the incessant, drumming, sodden rain part of what drove Reverend Davidson to suicide. He wouldn't have fallen to Sadie had it not been for the rain. And yet when my grandmother had to leave Arkansas for Arizona during the Great Depression, she told me: "I used to stand outside in the yard every day and look up at that clear blue sky and pray to God to send even just one cloud."

Monday, October 7
Fourth day of rain. I made eight 'eis this morning. I am keeping up Emily's gig with the Castaway for her while she is gone. We also went to the library this morning and I've been reading to the boys from Roald Dahl and Beatrix Potter. Now they're curled up on the couch on our veranda and we're all eating hot buttered toast. The rain comes off the roof in sheets and waterfalls. On the veranda we have water walls around us making the daylight green and liquid. There is a moment whenever we leave the house that we dash through those walls and emerge sputtering and drenched out in the spacious rain on the other side.

Tuesday, October 8
Fifth day of rain.

Wednesday, October 9
Sixth day of rain. There was a brief notice in the newspaper: "The recent rainfall began last Friday at about nine p.m. with light drizzle. The total amount

*of water that fell to eight the following morning was
1.3 cm. On Saturday 3.9 cm fell, Sunday 13.2 cm,
Monday 17.7 cm and yesterday from 8 a.m. to 2 p.m.—
4 cm." This does not seem right to me—not unless "cm"
stands for "buckets". We spent our afternoon peacefully
on the veranda—reading, listening to static-y ukulele
music on the radio, and playing dominoes.*

Thursday, October 10

*The seventh straight day of rain, although it
seems to be letting up some. We have been reading a
lot. Mostly we've been pretty happy. I'm perfectly
glad—at last—that we came here.*

Friday, October 11

*No rain today—sunny and breezy, with puffy
white clouds skidding across the sky. I seized the
opportunity and did our laundry, leaving it on the line
to dry while I took the kids to play in the park
by the market. We brought home Raro Fried Chicken
for lunch. In the evening we went to the movies in
town, holding hands in the murmuring dark of the
crowded cinema. Otherwise, we have not had much
contact with the outside world. I let Emily's phone
ring and ring and ring ... Emily Dickinson wrote,
"What indeed is Earth but a Nest, from whose rim
we are all falling." And if you're going to fall off*

the face of the Earth, the only thing to do is just let go.

I have noticed that my wristwatch has stopped working. Another happy day.

Saturday, October 12

I have received a letter out of the blue from Gregg, accusing me of heartlessness and cruelty for not having written to him. He has, he says, opened his mailbox every day for months anxiously expecting a message, and turned away from the empty box in despair. The fact is that even though I enjoy playing games of recrimination, guilt and pain as much as the next person, I can't be bothered thinking about him any more, not even to be cruel. I am much more interested in the life in front of me—in Aiden and Tris and the unconscious, singsong poetry of their talk, in the shells that wash up along the beach at high tide, in the moko that lives behind the bedside table in our room and is slowly growing a new tail to replace the one he has lost, in trying to avoid stepping on a cockroach barefoot in the dark.

You know you have lost your spell over a woman when she finds thinking about cockroaches more interesting than thinking about you.

I found a perfectly preserved crab shell on the beach. It even still had the fragile, clear eye membranes.

The boys invented a game called "Pukarua", about an ancient civilisation that was right next to the lost city of Atlantis. It had a flying train. Aiden made up strange and beautiful ritual chants as part of the ceremonies. These often involved sacrificing Tris to the gods, which Tris seemed to enjoy. One chant involved going into the mouth of heaven.

We went for drives on the back road, the Ara Metua, which has skirted the mountain's edge for a thousand years. Going through the valley one day, there were double rainbows arching over us. Into the mouth of heaven ...

We lived mostly on the veranda with books and toys, and breezes blowing through, and the smell of mosquito coils. The main toys were cushions from the chairs, from which the boys constructed houses, ships and racetracks.

Once the sun was back, we woke up with the wild roosters in our front yard. The boys climbed the guava and tipani trees outside our kitchen windows. We went down to the beach to build sand castles. We took drives to Wigmore's on the other side of the island to buy bread and candy bars and newspapers, just to drive along the sea. We saw almost no one—just Mata and Kali on Monday afternoons. Emily's phone hardly ever rang any more. We went to the library and the Bounty Bookstore. At night the boys fell asleep together in their big bed under the ceiling fan and I listened to them breathe and to the sound of the surf and the curious noise of palm trees.

Wednesday, October 30

    Aiden and Tris believe fervently in magic and by believing make it true. Their world is a constant delight, with expected charms raining down in answer to their imprecations, sometimes in surprising forms. Beautiful rocks, sparkly in the sunlight, and fantastic shells, broken into baroque shapes, inevitably find their way into their path. The leaves of the tipani trees whisper secrets only the chosen can hear, and the guava branches come alive, taking the boys for bucking rides on the ocean winds that the sea-god Tangaroa calls forth.

    The flowers they find are always beautiful and interesting, wafting down whenever they wait under the trees. While they watch, the cat makes miraculous leaps to the top of the bureau and the wild hens bring forth wondrous clutches of chicks, which they then parade past for review. When Mata takes the boys to feed the pigs, one of the sows has magically produced a litter of piglets.

    Aiden and Tris greet these outpourings of good fortune with inexhaustible delight. The gods could not shower their riches on two more grateful recipients. Despite living always inside a fantastic bubble of sea, sky and earth, despite having confident trust in never-ending magic, despite a daily parade of miracles that makes miracles ordinary, they never fail to be amazed.

Following along behind them in my grown-up skin of rationality, I feel miracles slip off them and flutter on to me like autumn leaves blown by the wind.

We were lucky to live where we did on the island because we were close to the main water line that came down from the reservoir. The closer you were to the water line, the more often you had water, and the more water pressure you had when you did have water. We almost always had water, even if water-of-a-sort. Whenever it rained the reservoir filled up with mud, and the water that came out of the tap was gritty and brown, and sometimes teemed even more than usual with animal life.

I had bought a water-purifier pump at a camping store in the US. It had a ceramic filter that could be scrubbed clean so the pump was reusable and would last us the whole year. I pumped litre after litre of water. It took about twenty-five squeezes to get a cupful. I was hoping that all the upper-body exercise would give me perky breasts like a nineteen-year-old, but no such luck.

Actually, the number of squeezes to fill a cup varied depending on the cleanliness of the ceramic filter core: the dirtier it was the more squeezes it took. Sometimes, when it had been raining hard, the water was so muddy

I had to clean the filter after pumping just one or two cups. The filter then had to dry for twenty-four hours before it could be used again, since the water with which I had cleaned it was also contaminated. So the more it rained, the less water we had.

After several days of slowly dehydrating in the midst of torrential rains, it finally occurred to me to catch the rainwater by putting all the soup kettles and big cooking pots out in the yard. Looking back, I am shocked it took me so long to figure this out.

What business does a person like me have thinking she should have children? It seems like a reasonable question, with all I've written so far about beer, and things I'm willing to put into my mouth, and how all I really want is to be left alone. Having children does not seem— for those seeking solitude—to be a reasonable plan to pursue. And make no mistake, I pursued these children passionately, with all my heart—the only true pursuit I have ever had. This is not the story of some drunken floozy who accidentally got knocked up and was too addled by religion or *Ladies' Home Journal* to find her way to the abortion clinic. I wanted those babies desperately, and I remember the very clear-sighted moment in the Cup A Joe coffee house in Raleigh, North Carolina, when I said to Eric, whom I only barely knew, "I want to have a baby."

He said, "I don't", and gave the standard speech about overpopulation that men of his ilk give. So I put all responsibility for birth control in his hands, or whatever. I was pregnant by the end of the summer.

I remember the night I went into labour. It was a little past midnight in late May. I lay alone in my bed, knowing it was time and watching the clock next to me, aware this was the last night I would ever spend alone—or at least for a long time. I remember saying goodbye to solitude, not regretfully but not joyfully either—just saying goodbye to something that had been part of me.

If you're looking for oblivion, kids are the ticket. Wake up every forty-five minutes for four months to breastfeed and you will no longer worry about anything having to do with you as a person. This is because you will not be a person per se, but only an approximation of one. You will be too tired to have a personal identity. Instead, you will have a sublime form of solitude: being alone with someone who is perfect for you because you made him. How could my children not be my soul mates when they were made out of the fiercest parts of my soul?

My wild and tumultuous babies! There are no vengeful gods. There is only the world we make for ourselves out of our passions.

I got long letters from Jonathan. Things continued to be grim in Switzerland. He was in mediation trying to set up the terms of his formal separation from his wife. She was clearly a piece of work: she had announced that her new career plan was to become a prostitute. This was from a forty-four-year-old woman running to fat. She had imparted the information while they were waiting outside the office of the divorce mediators. Jon was stunned. Did she actually believe someone would pay her for sex?

He was feeling blue. I wished I could bring him to the island and sit him down on the veranda, with a comforting view of the tipani trees and the wild chickens. I wasn't especially fond of the chickens, but they seemed to be strangely good for the soul.

The main road of Rarotonga circles the island for thirty-two kilometers, with impenetrable jungle on one side and endless ocean on the other. It takes about forty-five minutes to make the complete circuit, depending on how many motorbikes you have to pass, how many pass you, and whether or not you get stuck behind the bus. I got into the habit of taking the boys for a drive a couple of times a week, slowly circling the island for no particular reason. Tris and Aiden were always happy to go, sitting together in the back seat talking and laughing and watching the coconut trees slide by.

Partly we went because the car had air conditioning, and in the sweltering mid-afternoon heat the coolness was refreshing. Partly we went because the car had a tape player, and after the continual stream of ukulele music from the only radio station on the island it was refreshing to listen to something different. Partly, after a long time in our own secluded world, it was refreshing to get out and see other things. But I think the real reason we went was that I was memorising the island, every shop, rubbish bin, hand-lettered sign, tree, swerve and rock. Every atom of life. I was memorising it all, making it mine. It was my way of beginning to know this place, going over the same ground again and again and again.

By the time we left the island, we had driven two thousand miles.

Saturday, November 9

It's cooler today after three days of really sweltering weather—when I dropped the 'eis off at the Castaway, Cameron said it was 35 degrees Celsius on Thursday with 70 percent humidity. We went to the beach on Wednesday and Friday. It is lovely and cool floating on my back, half-submerged in the water. I have to be careful not to fall asleep and float off to Tahiti. There was a story in the newspaper last week about a tourist at the Rarotongan Beach Resort and Spa who managed to make it into open ocean while dozing on his inflatable raft. He was rescued by a fisherman who glimpsed him just as he was disappearing over the horizon. I would have thought the reef would have stopped him. Or the reef sharks.

Sharks can't make it inside the lagoon—it's mostly too shallow, especially at low tide, and the reef keeps them out. Tris swims around me in the gentle shallows, but the salt water stings Aiden's mosquito bites so he usually sits on rocks under the palm trees and reads. Sometimes he and Tris make big sandcastles with moats and fortifications right at the tide mark, battling bravely against the slow and steady onslaught of the sea. I have been telling them a story, "The Legend of the Golden Orb—Beware!", one episode each time we go to the beach. I lie in the water with my eyes closed and talk. The episode ends when I can't think of what would come next. This is usually at the height of the excitement. Right now the Armies of Light, who are disguised as dogs on Earth, have just breached the barrier between this world and the World of Darkness, where our heroes have been hopelessly trapped for quite some time. Whew. Then we cross the road to Fruits of Rarotonga and buy grilled cheese sandwiches and very melty ice cream.

Thursday was Mata's birthday. We gave her an electric fan. This is because Kali told me that Mata told her to tell me that's what she wanted.

Dad arrives tonight. Aiden is making him an 'ei of tipani blossoms, tiare māori and lime leaves.

MEN

My *father came to visit* for ten days in November, while Emily was away. I don't remember now how or when we had hatched the plan for his journey. It's a long way from Arkansas to Rarotonga—more than a day's flying—and he was just about to turn seventy. But he loves Aiden and Tris, his only grandchildren, and me so ardently that even that dreadfully long plane flight couldn't keep him away. Of all the people who joked about joining us, only my intrepid father ever really meant it.

We met him at the airport at two a.m. We had been clockless ever since my wristwatch stopped working, so for the occasion I had to buy an alarm clock at the CITC. When the plane landed, the boys were wild with joy, shrieking and throwing 'eis around my father's neck. We drove him to the Rarotongan Beach Resort and Spa (because even the most ardent love quails in the face of early morning aquatic worms) and he and the boys spent the night there in the air conditioning, while I slept at home in the strange stillness of the empty house. In the morning I went to get them, bringing all our empty water bottles to fill with the purified water of the hotel.

It was nice to have Dad with us. He saw how beautiful everything was instead of just how shabby. He loved the tipani trees, especially the ones with the white-yellow blooms, and was excited to find they were frangipani. He had long been singing the boys a song about a girl named Fan-Fan Fanny who lives under the frangipani. You could tell by the songs he sung that he was a child in New York City in the 1940s. We took him for a long walk along the beach to a place we called the Castle Rocks, where volcanic rocks tumbled across the sand into the water and made a cove that became everything in our imagination, harbouring pirate ships and lost cities and castles.

We took a drive along the back road, past the fields of banana trees and the taro swamps and the hedges thick with birds of paradise, and he said over and over again that this was the most exotic place he had ever been.

When I was little, my father had bought a piece of land in the Ozark foothills. We called it "the farm", but it was just some fields and piney woods and a stream. It was probably much stranger for my father to be on this land in Arkansas, having grown up in Brooklyn, than it was for me to be on Rarotonga, having grown up in Arkansas. I think he was drawn to that patch of wild unruly land by a need to be free from the chains of daily convention. There is a story about a time when my brothers and I were very young and our grandmother, my father's mother, was visiting us from New York. We were living in Arkansas, in the first house my father ever owned. My father was mowing the lawn and our grandmother was watching him. When he finished, he joined her on the porch, where she, the wife of a butcher, said to him, "But it's so *middle class*."

My father never mowed the lawn at home again, but on the farm he sometimes mowed a patch of pasture with an old push-mower. He had hacked down enough thistle and pigweed to make a small lawn, and on weekends he would haul rocks there for a house he was building. It was to be a round house made entirely of rocks from the farm. The wall got to be about three feet high with rocks stacked up on top of each other. Of course, it is awfully hard to build a house that way because it tumbles down, but for a long time I divided people into two camps: the ones who immediately said, when they heard about the house, "You can't build a house that way" and the people who saw the wild beauty of the idea. I felt then that I could only truly love the wild beauty people: thinking about tumbled-down walls showed a crippling lack of romance.

We did manage to build a low ring of rocks, put a grill on it, call it "the hearth" and cook beans and hot dogs. Once a hot rock exploded and once we saw a rattlesnake: those were the only real events that ever occurred. But beautiful nothings happened there all the time—days of light and shadow, wind and serenity. Sometimes we stopped on the way home in a little town called Lavaca and bought soft-serve ice cream dipped in chocolate. I wonder if, like me, my father has a thousand memories from those days, of children and sunshine and grass-hoppers and clouds, all jumbled together in a wordless kaleidoscope? Sometime during my teenage years, he sold the farm. Whatever it had been to him and to us, it was over by then.

In the Greek legend of Sisyphus, a wayward king is condemned to spend his life eternally pushing a rock up a hill. Camus wrote that "the struggle ... is enough to fill a man's heart. We must imagine him happy." Hauling warm rocks across a bit of wild heaven in Arkansas, maybe my father too had found the smiles of the earth.

Certainly all the reasons that Dad bought the farm and spent his weekends hauling rocks across the pasture were the same reasons he could look at our house on the island with no clean water, a rusty tin roof, wild chickens in the garden, moko hanging on the ceiling, and see how beautiful it all was. And, of course, the reason he had bought the farm in Arkansas was the same reason I had packed up my children and moved to the South Seas.

Like Camus's Sisyphus, I was now facing the curve of the gulf, the sparkling sea. Hadn't the boys and I also escaped the land of the dead?

Dad took Aiden and Tris off on the Raro Safari, a jeep trip that took tourists to see a waterfall in the interior of the island. I was supposed to take advantage of Dad's delight in his grandchildren to put in long productive afternoons of research but it was too hot. Instead I sat sweating on the veranda, and when they returned we went to the hotel to luxuriate in the air conditioning and swim in the pool. The girl at the reception desk recognised me. "Oh, you're back," she said, and seemed happy to see us, probably the result of some sort of professional hospitality training— either that or she had mistaken us for someone else. Now that I lived on the island I felt illegitimate snucking in my empty water bottles to fill and my piles of laundry to wash and dry in the coin-operated machines. Locals weren't supposed to go to the hotels. I tried to look somewhat vague and very American.

When Te Rangi Hiroa, the famous Maori anthropologist also known as Peter Buck, wrote his masterpiece about the Polynesians he called it *Vikings of the Sunrise*. When pioneering Polish anthropologist Bronislaw Malinowski wrote about the Melanesians, he called his book *Argonauts of the Western Pacific*. (*Argonauts* was wildly outsold by Malinowski's later—and surprisingly untitillating—work *The Sexual Life of Savages*, a marketing lesson for us all.) And the Cook Islanders' word for tribe or family clan is vaka—the same as their word for boat, the sort of graceful voyaging canoes on which, many centuries ago, Polynesians set out across the infinite ocean to populate every flyspeck atoll.

The early Pacific Islanders were not only great voyagers, but the greatest sailors the world has ever seen. Almost unimaginable bravery is required to push off from the shore of home and plunge across the reef into the heart of the tempestuous, misnamed Pacific in an open canoe with only stars to steer by and no known destination, knowing you may never come back, never see home again. Courage is not a small thing.

But there is more than one way to leave home. Dad left Brooklyn, New York in 1950, when he was seventeen. I once asked him if, when he died, he wanted me to take his ashes back to Brooklyn. He laughed and said, "God, no!" Just like when I told my grandmother that I was going to live in Italy. "What do you want to go there for?" she said. "We got out of there."

That doesn't necessarily mean, though, that it is easy to live the rest of your life far from home.

*

I ran into Ted at the library and he agreed to let me interview him. Ted was descended from the Makea Nui Ariki, or high chief, on his mother's side, but the tribe hadn't yet decided who would inherit the title—there were three other claimants. He was on his way home to the little cottage where he lived with his elderly father on the grounds of the palace.

The cottage was behind a high wall, and even though we walked by all the time I had never got more than a glimpse of it. It seemed ramshackle, beautiful and rather mysterious. I was hoping we would talk there, but we met instead at a café across the road. I waited for Ted in a front room that opened out to the road, but after he arrived we moved into a smaller room hidden away at the side. As we entered, a wooden sculpture in the corner called out, "Daddy!" I heard this perfectly clearly.

Ted and I talked for three hours—or rather Ted talked and I listened. His voice so mesmerised me that after I left I had a hard time remembering exactly what he had said. He seemed much bigger indoors than he did outside. I looked down at our bare feet near each other under the table and mine looked like a child's.

At one point Ted said, "I made that carving", tilting his head at the wooden sculpture. "I know," I said. "I heard it call out 'Daddy' to you when we came in."

"Daddy!" he snorted, with a wry laugh, as though the

sculpture were a teenager that had been giving him some trouble.

My father stayed with us for ten days. It was gloriously sunny the whole time, and then when he left it went right back to all day, every day rain again. By now the boys and I didn't notice the rain so much; if it kept us inside one day, there was always tomorrow, or the day after, or the day after that. Sometimes, though, if it had been raining since Tuesday when the plane landed, by Friday or Saturday we would see irritable-looking honeymoon couples sitting forlornly in cafés, looking out at the downpour instead of each other, bored with making love more quickly than they would have guessed possible and, from the look of them, questioning whether the marriage had been a good idea in the first place.

After he left, Dad sent an email to my brothers and their wives, telling them about the place where the boys and I now lived.

Dear Bill, Fran, Joe and Shelley,

Kathy wanted me to tell you what life was like on Rarotonga. It is a small island: you can see the ocean from almost any place. Except for the harbour, it is entirely surrounded by a reef, so no big waves. The beach is quite beautiful, clean, no people, beautiful palm trees, some great rock outcroppings, hibiscus and frangipani trees with white, pink, yellow and red flowers, and surrounds the entire island. Just inside, leaving various amounts of frontage (all public), a road goes around the whole island, takes about forty-five minutes, and most of buildings are on both sides of this. The interior is a small inactive (hah!) volcano surrounded by jungle, no real roads through, but passable and very lush, waterfalls, etc.

Kathy's house is in a compound owned by Emily, 82, widow, Catholic, wealthy landowner (only real source of wealth). The parcel is about twelve acres, goes to the ocean, with rental house close to the road and Emily's house back a-ways. It is about 3000 square feet, old and dilapidated, many rooms, all opening on to a veranda that surrounds the house, with a huge corrugated overhang. Not dark inside because some of roof is translucent plastic (good for hurricanes). Kathy's part is connected but at one corner: bedroom, bath and kitchen. All activities take place on veranda, quite secluded. Yard contains palm, frangipani, breadfruit, guava, lime, passionfruit, apple, hibiscus, coconut, etc. just for the picking, and pawpaw, which we call papaya, and all bloom most of the year.

It was warm when I left, the beginning of their summer and hurricane season, but the ocean and sky and beach and flora are magnificent and the weather was great. There are flame trees, which at Christmas

produce red flowers that look like fire. Also fan palms
and many butterflies. There is none, little or erratic:
air conditioning, TV, telephone, fresh meat, treated
water. There are, in abundance: mokos (five-inch
lizards), rats, mynah birds, starving dogs (Kathy says
convicted Nazi war criminals get their comeuppance by
coming back to life as Cook Island dogs), wild chickens
and roosters. Only fourteen thousand Māori, with
another fifty-eight thousand living in New Zealand
because of lack of jobs on the island. One hundred and
fifteen percent of the population are members of
churches. We went to Catholic mass: Māori music, very
moving. One grocery market and a few small stores.
Many unfinished buildings: ran out of money or funds
dribbling back from New Zealand; also land disputes.
No lawyers but disputes solved, not quickly, by
genealogists. Missionaries did nothing good. Did not
influence moral attitudes; did screw up centuries-
old land customs, hence the disputes and hence the
poverty. The people bury their dead in the front yard,
interesting reflection on the idea of land. Kathy must
shop every day because most foods do not last, even in
the refrigerator. Kids swim every day and find places to
play around the beach, trees and rocks to climb. Kathy's
work proceeding, boys brown and healthy.

Love, Dad

Soon after my father left I started to see a lot of Nate Flynn around town, running into him at the grocery store or the bookstore or the bank. Because lots of people had known about me from my official application to conduct research, which had apparently been circulated widely, lots of people I met called me Katherine, my official application-to-conduct-research name. Nate called me Katherine, always with a note of pleased surprise when he spotted me standing with the boys by the Sanitarium cornflakes or wherever. We would have a strained, bashful conversation, advancing towards each other and then retreating, like waves washing the shore, and although in the first few seconds it always seemed he was happy to see me, I was never certain from minute to minute whether or not he really was. I had heard from others about his beautiful, angry wife and their sadly stormy marriage, but this was long before things between them became, as they eventually did, intolerable.

Right after Dad left, the boys and I went to another opening at Kay George's gallery. The room was sweltering, jammed with people, and I spent most of the evening standing outside in the cool talking to Nate. He told me that for a long time he had made paintings he didn't show to anyone: he kept them in a shed in his back garden.

"Were you shy or embarrassed?" I asked him. "No, it wasn't that," he said, looking off into the dark. "It was that

I was free. I was free, making things that I didn't have to show to anyone. I made them just for me and didn't have to give a damn about anyone else."

Listening to him talk, standing next to him in the dark with the loud hot party swinging behind us, made me feel almost giddy.

Monday, November 25

It's pouring—absolutely pouring—with rain today. Sometimes it's so loud we have to shout to be heard over the sound of it on the roof. I find it comforting, and actually I am in need of comfort. First, a cockroach flew in the door and landed right on me. Cockroaches are bad enough without flying. They are bad enough just lying around on their backs dead in the far corners of cabinets. I thought there might be something that would eat cockroaches, maybe moko or the cat, something kind of furry and cute. But now it seems we have an infestation of brown hairy spiders that are bigger than my hand. When I wished for something to eat the cockroaches, I have to say I wasn't quite expecting that.

Aiden was sitting in bed reading last night when one of them crawled right out from behind the headboard and headed up the wall towards the ceiling. After first having a heart attack and dying, I ran for Emily's can of bug spray and gave us all cancer by

spraying a couple of gallons on to the spider, which
proved to be remarkably resilient and made it all the
way into the middle of the bathroom floor before the
bug spray ran out and I smashed it with the empty
can. When it finally died—either from the poison or
the smashing or the piercing sonic vibrations of Aiden,
Tris and I all screaming our heads off—it released an
egg sac and, triggered no doubt by some goddamn
miracle of nature, twenty billion baby spiders
immediately emerged from the sac and moved with
remarkable speed in every direction, dispersing
themselves throughout the house while I could only
gape at them, stunned.

I am wondering how long, in this climate, it
takes twenty billion baby spiders to grow from the size
of pinheads to the size of Hitchcock stars. Given that a
pepper seed I dropped by the back steps last month is
already a foot-high plant producing new peppers, I'm
betting not long. Now every time something brushes
against my bare skin, I jump about three feet.

Jonathan wrote me long letters, sometimes composed
over the course of days and days.

Hey beautiful,
Goddamit, I can't find the longish letter I
finished yesterday. I may have to go to the basement

and dig through the bins of paper that go out to
recycling. It's possible that I threw out the stack of
really important stuff (like a letter to you and overdue
bills to pay) when I was "organising" my office
yesterday. Whatever, I'm here in my office again.

He sounded a bit down. He also seemed to think I
would be coming to Zürich to see him—as if it were
settled, that the boys and I would be there with him.

The sun has gone behind Ütliberg, a big hill
(almost a small mountain) to the west of the city of
Zürich. It's getting cooler. When you come here, we
will all go up to the top of Ütliberg. There is a train
that goes most of the way; you then get out and, after
stopping for a while at a pretty nice playground, walk
to the very top, where there is a restaurant (ice cream
for the kids, or barley soup if it's cold, espresso for
addicts like me) with a view of the distant high alps,
weather permitting. On the walk between the summit
and the train station, there is often someone selling
chestnuts he roasts on a fire that he builds right there.
In Rome, when you buy chestnuts, they give them to
you in a cone of rolled newsprint. Here they have boxes
of strange double cones and they fill one of the cones
with the chestnuts. It took me ages to figure out that
the second cone is for the shells, so you won't litter.

I learned that through finally understanding a "helpful" local who was yelling at me for throwing my shells on the street.

I couldn't imagine anything further removed from Rarotonga. It was odd to think of a place where the ocean wind didn't sweep everything clean in the night, where people yelled at you for littering the street, or where, for that matter, there were streets on which to litter. I wasn't sure I would like Switzerland.

Public transportation is great here. Like Italy under Mussolini, everything runs on time ...

Like Italy under Mussolini, I doubted being "on time" was really worth it.

He had been working twenty-hour days in an attempt to keep from dwelling too much on the end of his marriage. It was doing wonders for his career, at least.

I could be working I guess, but I've had a lousy day so I'm spoiling myself by writing to you instead. One nice thing about staying so long at work two nights ago was that when I pulled up on my bike in front of my new apartment at nearly four a.m., there was a large and beautiful fox who calmly looked me over and then disappeared into the bushes. There are

*lots of foxes in Switzerland, even in the cities. In the
urban ecosystems of northern Europe they play the
role that raccoons play in the US and feral cats play in
southern Europe—all those wild cats in Rome, for
example. The one I saw the other night had long
gorgeous fur and several bands of different shades
along its tail.*

I remembered being in Rome with Jonathan fifteen
years before, right before we broke up, but my memory
was only in shades of grey. The places we'd been weren't
real to me any more. Only the fox seemed real.

Once I started getting mail, I heard from Jonathan
fairly frequently. No matter how dreadful his marriage had
been, the end was not proving easy. And he was lonely in
Switzerland. He hadn't wanted to go there and had agreed
only in a last-ditch effort to save his marriage. I think at
first he had started to write to me just because I was the last
good thing he could remember, the last time he had been
happy with someone. And I wrote him back because, even
after all those years, he was still a part of me. I hadn't ever
stopped thinking about him.

November is springtime in the southern hemisphere, and
Rarotonga, which had seemed so fragrant and flower-
filled even in August, now fairly exploded with blossoms.
In late November, the island held the Miss Tiare beauty

pageant, in which each contestant was represented by a different flower—Miss Hibiscus, Miss Tipani, Miss Tiare Māori and so on. The next week it hosted Miss South Pacific, which rotated through the participating countries from year to year. The boys and I watched the Miss South Pacific float parade in town one Saturday morning. This didn't happen on purpose, but when there is only one road and a parade is happening on it and you (not knowing a parade is about to start) have parked your car off to the side of it while you are in the post office and the bookstore, you watch the parade. There were seven contestants, one each from Fiji, the Cook Islands, Hawai'i (which is in the North Pacific, but we do not quibble), Tuvalu and Tonga, and two from Samoa—Miss Samoa and Miss American Samoa.

It was interesting to see how Western tourism had changed the conception of beauty. Miss Hawai'i was a fragile-looking girl with skinny arms and a big Pepsodent smile. Tuvalu, on the other hand, has few tourists, and Miss Tuvalu was happily and generously proportioned. A newspaper story about the parade said she "surprised the crowd at the Punanga Nui Market with her dancing skills." I bet she did. I'm surprised right now just thinking about it, and I didn't even go to the market.

I wish now that I *had* gone. According to the same article Miss Cook Islands walked over the bodies of the warriors who accompanied her. They lay face down on the ground, which must have been none too comfortable, but they were probably glad that at least it wasn't Miss Tuvalu.

My favorite in the parade was Miss American Samoa. That was one big young woman, not round and chubby like Miss Tuvalu but *big*. She was maybe six feet two, and had enough reach and heft to make her right hook formidable.

I saw Nate Flynn in the crowd watching outside Trader Jack's, but I didn't talk to him because lately, whenever I got close to him, I had a hard time breathing properly.

It was very quiet after dinner. When the sun set our house would seem all alone in the lilac pool of night. After washing the dishes, I would walk barefoot down our long dirt drive with our little bag of table scraps and paper napkins to put it in the rubbish bin, an old oil drum, by the edge of the road. From there I could see how high the tide was and watch the stars come out over the ocean. The beach hibiscus was just at the foot of the drive and late every afternoon it would start to drop all its flowers, so that by evening the drive was sprinkled with blossoms, pale translucent yellow at first, but gradually turning darker and redder until finally they were flame-coloured. The petals were delicate, like moth wings. I walked as carefully as I could between them when I went back up to the house so as not to crush them, but by morning they were always gone, faded into nothingness.

The light from our window looked warm and golden. I could hear Aiden's small voice and then Tris's even smaller one coming from inside, like the sound of katydids at dusk. I walked back up the driveway and across the garden towards the light, listening to their delicate, faraway sound and knowing they were there waiting for me, and that I was coming home to them.

At night I carefully locked up the house, closing the tall double-doors and carefully latching them. I shut the louvred door from the veranda into our little makeshift kitchen, with our electric tea kettle and our toaster and our one-burner hot plate, and made sure that it was tight, even though it had no lock. Then I locked the door between our room and the rest of the house with the large silver key that stayed in our side of the lock, and pulled tight the door leading from our room to the veranda, latching it at the top and the bottom.

I was never frightened, all alone in our secluded glen, just the boys and I in the dark night. Maybe I should have been, although what good it would have done I don't know.

In the mornings when I got up, I went around the house and opened everything wide again so the ocean breeze flowed through and washed away the night.

It is hard to write about happiness—at least, without

sounding like a liar. It's almost impossible to make clear the transcendent joy of taking out the trash every evening, so I only occasionally sent group emails now. The people to whom I was sending them had started to seem like phantoms, faded into unreality by time and distance. Dad was still real and Jonathan was still real. They were the only two. My life was made up of Aiden and Tris, Mata and Kali, Cameron and Dorothy at the Castaway Beach Villas, the clerks at the CITC and the post office, Johnny at the library, Kay George and Nate Flynn and a handful of other artists. Summer began to unfold and weeks of hot hazy days slipped by before I could muster up the energy to contact the outside world again.

Monday, December 2
Kia orana everyone,

I hope you are all doing well. I haven't written in a while but not much has been happening. The hurricane season has started and the government is likely to fall soon. Both of these events, though, are much less exciting on a day-to-day basis than they look written down like that and neither requires much action from me. In order to be a responsible citizen, however, I buy the newspaper more often than I might otherwise, and I did look at the Hurricane Preparation section in the front of the phone book. Stage One of Hurricane Preparation—"Tie your roof to the base of nearby trees"—so flummoxed me I decided to eschew Hurricane Preparation and rely entirely on dumb luck.

Reading the newspaper has been equally helpful. These are two sample items, both of which appeared last week. The first is headlined "Aging Hippie Artists Prompt Terrorism Rumours in Samoa":

> Apia, Nov 11—A group of well-heeled but aging hippie artists who have taken over a Samoan resort for a year have sparked Pacific-wide rumours, strongly denied on Monday, that Muslim terrorists were building a base there. Samoa is an avowed Christian state with little experience of other religions or lifestyles and the artists' yoga exercises have led to speculation that they are Muslims. "They have actions which appear as if they are worshipping Allah, but no, their actions are for exercise," Sinalei Resort owner Folasaitu Annandale told Televise Samoa.

The second is from a weekly column, "Ask Aunty Pati". (You need to know that an umu is a traditional underground cooking pit. An umukai is a feast made in the umu.)

> Dear Aunty Pati, I think my neighbours are stealing my dogs. Every time we get a puppy and it gets big, it disappears. Shortly afterwards, our neighbours have an umu. Should I call the police?
> Dog Lover

Dear DL, It probably wouldn't do any good to call the police because most of them were probably at the umukai. If you need help or information on being a responsible dog owner, contact the people at the Esther Honey Animal Clinic. They will be pleased to help you with tips and advice on training.

We have been to a few umukai and I make it a point to remain ignorant of the meat. I think of it as "mixed grill", which sounds so much tastier than "poodle".

Okay, enough of that. Well, just one more headline: "Public Demands Larger Seats to Accommodate Polynesian Backsides".

The breadfruit, alas, are in high season and dropping like neutron bombs all over the yard. We're eating them out of self-defence if nothing else. The traditional way of preparing breadfruit is to pound it into a mush with an ironwood mallet. (This is considered men's work and possession of a large breadfruit mallet is supposed to be quite an enticement to women.) Then you bury the mush in a pit and let it ferment for a month or two. It tastes, unfortunately, precisely as you would imagine. Instead, I'm making a sort of French fry out of them—proving that everything tastes better if you cook it in butter and dredge it in salt. We are

hampered only by an unfortunate lack of ketchup—
the ketchup boat having sunk in a storm off Fiji.

So what with the breadfruit and Muslim hippie
yoga terrorists and all, I decided to take the boys to
safety on one of the outer islands for a while. We went
to Aitutaki, our nearest neighbour, just a couple of
hundred miles away. After a breathtaking (in a couple
of different ways) flight over the world's most
iridescent lagoon, we landed at the Aitutaki airport—
a thatch-roofed hut at the end of a World War II
crushed-coral landing strip with a hand-lettered
wooden sign, "Welcome to Aitutaki". There are plans
afoot to pave the runway, which will definitely take
some of the sport out of it.

The relatively small distance from Rarotonga to
Aitutaki doesn't begin to measure the enormous space
between them. Aitutaki is impossibly beautiful and
strangely desolate—so quiet that coming back to Raro
was shocking. All that will end next month when
Aloha Airlines starts a direct flight to Aitutaki from
Honolulu. The Mormons have already sent an advance
guard of missionaries.

Culture in Aitutaki still has remarkably little
Western influence, although at dinner one night we
were serenaded by a cover band playing "Mustang
Sally" on conch shell and wooden drum. I bought a
couple of tapes of local music. (Our rental car has a

tape player and air conditioning—a little blue
America on wheels.) The Kaimer Experience String
Band tape features a cover photo of the five band
members dressed only in leaves and smiles, but when
they launched into their version of "If I Said You Had a
Beautiful Body, Would You Hold it Against Me?" I
knew Cook Islanders had perfected the ukulele as an
instrument of torture.

The best singing goes on in the churches, with
incredible a capella Polynesian harmonies
miraculously and spontaneously produced by the
whole congregation. Emily and I both have a crush on
the local priest, Father Kevin, so we sometimes attend
mass together. The women here wear white hats
woven from pandanus leaves and carry matching fans
attached to pearl shell handles. I have, as you all
know, never been one to pass up the opportunity to
make a fashion statement and now appear on Sunday
mornings with an enormous white hat and fan,
lacking only a fluffy tail to look like some crazed
duchess from "Alice in Wonderland". It is unclear
whether God is any more attentive to my prayers, but
at least I have not yet been struck down by lightning.

The flame trees are starting to bloom and the
pineapples are getting ripe—a sure sign of Christmas—
but even for a southerner it's too balmy and bright
blue to feel right. The boys and I sit sweating under

the ceiling fan singing "Rudolf the Red-Nosed
Reindeer" and as much of "Winter Wonderland" as
I can remember. When I run out of the lyrics, I
improvise. The boys squint suspiciously at me, but
I look innocent.

Kia manuia, Kathy

Beginning in late November I didn't hear from Jonathan for a long while. On Monday afternoons, while Mata was minding Aiden and Tris, I would dash into the Telecom office to send a quick email to my father before heading off to interviews with artists. Often there would be an email or two from Jonathan and I would send him something back, but the emails stopped coming around the time I got the letter about the foxes.

At first, I didn't think too much about it—I knew he was busy at work. But after a few weeks I started to have the feeling he might have found some closer consolation than an old girlfriend half a world away. He was a very sweet guy, after all, and I had had to fight off plenty of competitors when I first wooed him twenty years before. I tried to be glad that he had, as I assumed, found someone more interesting than me. I tried not to be jealous, which would have been ridiculous in the circumstances. I imagined him happy, which is what we should all want for the people we love, right?

The library was my favorite place on the island. It was a small white building sitting at the end of a garden and shaded by flame trees and palms. It had two rooms—one for the library and one for the museum (admission $1), with an alcove for the children's book section in the middle. There were never more than one or two other people. I had started to make friends with the librarian, Johnny. Johnny had been in the movies with her sisters in the 1950s, dancing the hula on a Hollywood soundstage minus their belly buttons: the movie executives had made them tape over them and paint the tape to match their skin so as not to shock the Americans. I hadn't ever seen Johnny's belly button but I couldn't imagine I would be more shocked by the sight of it than I would by the sight of someone who had no belly button at all. There were echoes of the Renaissance painters fretting over whether or not to depict Adam and Eve with navels—thus all those paintings with Eve's genitalia in full view and her midsection discreetly covered by foliage. There were serious theological implications at stake.

Johnny let Aiden take out the THIS BOOK IS NOT TO BE REMOVED FROM THE LIBRARY books and once gave us a bunch of bananas. There was a lovely wood and brass card catalogue filled with faded cards bearing only a tenuous connection to the actual book collection. There were bowls of gardenias at the tall wooden counter that Aiden could just barely peep over when he checked out books. The books had cards in pockets on their inside back covers. The cards got stamped with the due date and then filed in an old cigar box under the counter. There were no computers, no bar codes, just the Dewey Decimal System and slowly revolving ceiling fans and books whose pages I turned very carefully so they wouldn't disintegrate in my hands.

On Tuesday afternoons, there was story hour out on the lawn for the little kids. We went every week—it was the most disciplined thing we did. Aiden and I would sit next to each other at one of the long wooden tables and read, while Tris's voice floated in through the window during the part of story hour when the children sang.

The ceiling in the museum was being repainted one Tuesday, and after the story hour Tris and I went in to have a look at all the different kinds of crabs, carefully laid out on sand in a glass-topped display case, with an identification label next to each one. It was wonderful and a little spooky to be in this dusky museum crammed with fantastic objects, with the lights off and sheets draped everywhere and the late afternoon sun unfolding through the windows. I wondered who had put the crabs in the case. Who in the dusty long ago had spread the sand and carefully laid out the specimens between pieces of pretty coral and smooth-polished stones? Were they ghosts now, hovering somewhere, watching us? Or were they only dust, sitting in the graveyard just past the far end of the library garden?

Would they smile to see us now, Tris in all his grave serenity, contemplating the spotted pebble-crab (*Carpilius maculatus*) and the big dead shell of the coconut crab (*Birgus latro*)? Was some silent spirit shocked to find the reef shoes he had woven out of palm leaves in fifteen minutes one summer morning, thinking to catch an octopus for lunch, displayed with due consequence in the large glass case, a paragraph of explanatory text appended? What would the carver of the three-legged coconut scraper think to find us standing in front of it in silent contemplation? They, whoever they were, were now only ghosts or dust and their traces left behind in the shadows. Some day Tris and I would be ghosts or dust, without even a display of crabs left behind to mark our hazy afternoon.

I began to run into Nate Flynn in town more and more frequently. His name sounded to me like an eighteenth-century British sailor. There was certainly one somewhere in his ancestry—or a pirate, more likely—but he was so gigantic and dark there weren't many visible traces of Olde Britannia left—except for his dark blue eyes. Sometimes we would talk for a long time. The more I talked to him, the more I found myself wanting to make art, rather than just write about it.

One day I got out my camera and took some pictures of a tuna fish we had bought that morning by the side of the road in Arorangi, a village on the west coast of the island. The boys helped by forcibly restraining the cat, who was too enamoured of the tuna to be supportive of artistic creation. Afterwards, I hacked the tuna apart with the sharpest kitchen knife I could find and baked some steaks in Emily's oven for our lunch, and some to take to Mata, who didn't have an oven. I saved the head for Mata (she used them to make soup) and then gave all the rest to the cat. She was joyous. Now she was my faithful slave forever. Or twenty minutes, whichever came first.

As well as frequenting the library, we got books at the Bounty Bookshop in town. The sign featured a full-masted eighteenth-century British sailing ship so you would know that "Bounty" was a historic reference to mutiny, misery and lost souls. It was a small shop tucked into a corner by the post office. One wall had a rack of maps and guidebooks, mostly of the Cooks and other places in the South Pacific. One wall had magazines from New Zealand and the sorts of books you find in airport newsstands—lightweight spy thrillers and tame romance novels. There was a rack of children's books in the middle of the room and some shelves with office supplies and airmail stationery. Finally, there was an alcove with miscellaneous five-and-dime toys—balloons and cheap Halloween masks, fragile plastic baby dolls and toy trucks, dusty Frisbees and disheartened bath boats.

After checking for mail we would stop by to buy the *Cook Islands News* from the stack on the counter if there were any left: they were usually sold out by mid morning. We also bought books. I still have some of them, Little Golden Books that we bought for Tris, slightly faded as though they had been waiting for us for a long time, and other books I'd never heard of before and have never come across anywhere since. There were also unusual technical manuals and charts. I bought one called *Tropical Forage Legumes* because of its beautiful drawings of plants, and tables such as "Table 14.12: Growth rhythm of *Stylosanthes humilis* in Northern Australia".

For the first couple of months we loaded up with these treasures, but I began to notice after a while that new books rarely appeared, even when the boat had obviously come because CITC's shelves were groaning with cans of mackerel from Japan and corned beef from New Zealand. The bookshelves got emptier and emptier until finally Tris had every Little Golden Book there was and I had even bought a ragged copy of *Temptation I$land* ("The dark side of paradise").

When I was growing up in Arkansas, I remember only one bookstore. It was not much bigger than the Bounty Bookshop, and on visits my father would always buy us whatever we wanted. However, the real source of books was Dad's study. Bookcases covered the walls from floor to ceiling, and I would spend countless afternoons hanging my head upside down off the sofa and reading in the curtained gloom, roaming my way through Steinbeck and Hemingway and Isherwood and Kazantzakis. Even as small children, my brothers and I were allowed to read anything we wanted—with the single exception of James Joyce's *Finnegans Wake*, which was strictly forbidden, placed out of reach on the highest shelf. There was a reason, even if an eccentric one. Dad was afraid, he said, that if I read *Finnegans Wake* I would never read another book. Its being forbidden was no doubt part of Dad's plan to get me to read a very difficult but wonderful piece of writing. Certainly it gave the book a powerful allure. I memorised the first page because I thought it was so beautiful. I still have the book, with "Paul Leo Giuffre, Brooklyn, N.Y." written inside in my father's handwriting.

Sunday, December 8

Damn, it's hot. It's after midnight and still damn hot. The boys are asleep but I've finally abandoned all hope and come out on the veranda. Such a sultry liquid night makes me think of William Blake—"Bring me my arrows of desire." I'm feeling like Saint Sebastian now, with arrows of desire. This is absurd: I'm sitting under the hot tropical moon, listening to the throbbing pulse of the surf in the lagoon, smelling the perfume of the night-blooming cereus, and feeling like a spinster or a nun. What kind

of a person comes to a lovers' paradise and neglects to
take a lover? An idiot.

By early December, it was full-blown summer and it seemed to me I'd always lived on the island. I thought about Nate Flynn sometimes during the long hot nights, but I really wasn't looking for that kind of trouble. I was happy enough for the time being.

Then on the second Monday of December, when Mata showed up to take care of Aiden and Tris, I rushed to the post office to check my email and found a message from Jonathan that had been waiting for me almost a week. It was scrambled and mostly incoherent.

> *sorry about the typing, my left hande doesn't*
> *really wellllork (I ust spent a week in the ICU after*
> *bouncing my skull off the street on the way to the*
> *climbing gym by bike last Saturday*

He was in a rehabilitation clinic in Switzerland. He asked me to call him.

> *is there no phone number that might ork for*
> *you? I have a numbe for EMily, and I wasw about*
> *to start buhgging her, also I thought ogf calling your*
> *father, exvcept I don't*
> > *know if he would release any information*
> *to me...*

*perhap you are hard to get in touh with becasue
you don't want a zillion visitors. I had thought of
trying to stop in at some time around Xmas or in
Febrary if that waw OK with you, but my swiss ER doc
would probably not like that plan*

*gotta go to bed, my head hurts. Hope you and
your boys are haing fun, muh love, jonathan*

I waited until late in the evening—there was a twelve-hour time difference—and then used Emily's telephone to call him. He sounded okay but he couldn't remember anything at all about the day of the accident. He had been unconscious in Intensive Care for a week. He couldn't remember much about that week either, only fuzzy bits here and there. We couldn't talk for long—the Swiss nurses were yelling at him to hurry because he was late for his relaxation exercises. I promised to call again soon.

COMPANY

Towards *the end of the year*, our days of reclusive isolation ended. We expected Emily back sometime after Christmas and Mata started coming by the house on more than just Monday afternoons. She was supposed to have been taking care of the yard while Emily was away, and now leapt into belated action, hacking back the encroaching jungle and raking the rambling garden into tidiness.

I started calling Jonathan every now and then, and I also started answering the phone, always hoping it was him. Sometimes it was, but usually it was a friend of Emily's, checking if she was back yet. After finding out that she wasn't, they would chat with me instead. And around the island, we had friends now: Kay George at her gallery, where we would stop by in the mornings; Johnny at the library, where it was cool and quiet in the afternoons; Nate Flynn, almost. Of all the white faces that passed through the Telecom and the CITC and the Bounty Bookstore, most were here for ten days and then gone again. We had become members of the tiny cast who stayed on and so it took us a long time now to run our errands because we talked with everyone along the way—news and gossip (which are the same thing on a small island) and the intricate concerns people share when they are stranded alone together far away in the middle of the sea. Then, sometime in late November or early December, Fiona came to the island to stay for five months.

I met Fiona first in Kay George's gallery, but I met her again the following week in the cold room at the CITC. She was English and had arrived with her two children. She was a single mom too, and a photographer. We talked for a long time, standing there by the limes and the fresh milk, about being on our own with children. She told me about a man she had dumped recently when he became enraged at her, storming in from her garden bellowing, "Where is the two-handled axe? Why can't I find the two-handled axe!"

"What is a two-handled axe?" I asked.

"I have no idea," she said, laughing.

When I think about Fiona now, I think of her laughing. She kept popping up places. I remember her sitting with her children, Alma and Oskar, in the Maitai Café, where I had sat so often with Aiden and Tris during our first weeks on the island, and calling hello as I went past on my way to the Telecom office one Monday afternoon, her curly blonde hair like a sunburst in the café's dim, cool interior. I remember her browsing in the books at the Bounty Bookshop, pleased to find the strange charts and old agricultural manuals to which I had become so inured.

"Have you seen this?" she would chirp, delighted.

"Um, yes," I'd say. "Yes, I have."

Late one night I telephoned Jonathan from Emily's phone. It was raining heavily and I was sitting in Emily's big chair in her workroom with water thundering on the tin roof; I held the phone out so he could hear the roar. It was hot dark night for me, surrounded by the tropical monsoon, sitting in the warm yellow glow of a dangling light bulb high above my head, with moko hunting by its light. It was cold morning for him, half a world away in a sterile Swiss clinic with frosty Swiss people chivvying him around. He sounded very lonely. He would be well enough soon to go to his parents' house in New Jersey for a while. It had been almost a month since his accident.

I turned forty on December 20. It was a lovely, sunny, wild rose day. I woke up with the boys in my bed where they had migrated in the middle of the night, so the three of us were squashed together while the wide, blue-sheeted expanse of their bed lay rumpled and deserted. Aiden read me the birthday poem he had written: "Mom, mom, you're really great / And you're never late!" I made four 'eis in the morning and then we went to the library. I bought a copy of *To Kill a Mockingbird* from the selection of used books because I liked the library so much and wanted to do that on my birthday. I talked to Johnny about our coming trip to Easter Island, then we went to the beach and swam and ate popsicles at Fruits of Rarotonga. Back home I let the boys unwrap one Christmas present each. I was sitting on the veranda, drinking a glass of champagne and feeling that there weren't words enough for this kind of bliss when I spotted Elder Smith and Elder Winston coming up the drive for an impromptu visit. The champagne had made me uncharacteristically relaxed and chatty. I was very welcoming, much more so than religious proselytisers expect. We never saw them again.

I'm older now of course, older than when I celebrated my fortieth birthday in a place that now seems so far away, so long ago. I have a picture taken on my birthday, one of the very few of me from that year because usually I was the one holding the camera. I am sitting in the dappled sunshine on the veranda steps, wearing a white dress and a crown of tipani blossoms from the trees in our garden. The dress is Emily's, borrowed from an open closet in one of the unused bedrooms. My arms and shoulders are burnt brown. I have put on lipstick and my lips are dark red.

If life is measured in seasons, this is my summertime. The torrential storms of spring are over and the lashing rains of fall haven't come yet. Winter is an unfathomable world away. The woman sitting in the pool of warm light is a moment out of a long stretch of summer. I look at her and can't believe she is me. Maybe if I had stayed on the island, it would have stayed summer forever. I would have stayed summer forever.

Emily did just that. I asked to take her picture one day, and before she let me she went out into the garden and plucked a hibiscus flower to put behind her ear. I have that picture too. Putting the pictures side by side, it is clear that the woman on the veranda steps with the tipani blossoms in her hair is very much the daughter of the fragile woman with the scarlet hibiscus behind her ear. I look at the picture and can't remember what it was like to have brown arms and red lips.

But maybe the picture is a lie, an image of summertime serenity that I constructed for my birthday because I felt it was the way it should have been. Looking at my journal now, there was never a time when there weren't storms, thunder, floods. I begin to wonder if it really rained as much as I thought it did. Or maybe the storms were only inside me.

Sunday, December 22
Just at the end of the rain the tops of the volcanoes appeared above the mist and the clouds—

pale grey against paler grey, like imagined things,
spirits protecting the town below.

The weather became much wilder as the height of summer approached. One day the tide was terrifically high, much higher than the highest tide I had ever seen. The boys and I went for a walk along the beach to the Castle Rocks. We had made this walk scores of times before, Aiden and Tris running ahead of me across the smooth sand, laughing and never waiting for me to catch up while they called back to me and their faint, happy voices got carried away on the wind. The lagoon was usually tranquil and sparkling turquoise, and we knew every rock, tree and curve of beach. Now, though, the world was awash. All the familiar places had been transformed by brown water foaming and flooding up on to the beach and into the palm groves near the shore. At a place where usually a tiny stream trickled down between two shallow banks and spread a miniature delta across the sand, there was now a mighty surge of sandy ocean water.

I carried Tris on my hip, with one arm hard around him. With the other hand I held tight to Aiden's little hand. Even beyond the old high-tide mark the water was above my knees, almost to Aiden's waist, warm and foamy and dark. We sloshed along over the submerged beach where always before the sand had been only gently tickled by the surf. The Castle Rocks were now lonely little islands. I hoisted the boys up on the nearest one. They stretched their arms in the wind like wings, and together we looked out towards the churning sea.

The next day was Christmas. Aiden, Tris and I had decorated a palm tree in a pot on our veranda to put presents under. The boys each got a remote-control car I had purchased surreptitiously from the Bounty Bookshop, and drove them around on the veranda. We had Christmas dinner at the house of Mata's boyfriend, Rupert, in Tupapa with Mata, Rupert, Kali and Kali's parents. I had met Kali's mother once before but this was the first time I had met her father. When we arrived at 10.30 in the morning, he and Rupert were already drunk, sitting outside at the back of the house with a bottle of Jack Daniels each and a case of beer on the ground between them.

We exchanged presents. With a sense of cultural imperialist guilt, I handed Kali the Barbie she had requested. She had asked me the week before if any people on the island I came from had brown skin. She had once had white skin, she said, but it had turned brown because she played in the sun so much. Then we waited for the umukai to be ready. Mata had been up since dawn husking drinking coconuts because she knew how much I liked them. There was a small mountain waiting.

Usually, an umu is made by digging a pit in the yard, putting in firewood, and placing lots of black volcanic rocks on top. You light the fire, and by the time the wood burns down the rocks are very hot. You then put the food—chicken, taro, rukau and fish wrapped in banana leaves—on the rocks, add more banana leaves and cover the whole thing with dirt. The food slowly cooks for hours and then you take it out.

The umu at Rupert's house, however, was not like this. It was made out of a broken-down washing machine in the garden. The hot rocks were at the bottom and the food was wrapped in banana leaves on the top. It saved having to dig a hole, Rupert said.

Mata had made a feast. There were even sea cucumber intestines, which are considered—for unknown reasons—a delicacy. Sea cucumbers look like big turds lying lethargically in the warm shallow water. You pick them up, forcibly repressing fifty thousand years of evolutionarily hard-wired repugnance towards handling shit, slit them open, pull out the intestines, and throw the bodies back in the water. This doesn't kill the sea cucumbers: they are able to regenerate. I imagine it does startle them quite a bit though.

Having learned a lesson about the culinary properties of the gastrointestinal tract from having eaten tripe twenty years earlier, I declined the sea cucumber. Kali's father was already making beerily belligerent rumblings in my direction and my refusal of the guts finally sent him over the edge. "You Americans," he yelled, "you don't know what is good for you. These"—he shook a forkful in my face—"these are filled with protein!"

I sweetly pointed out that *he* wasn't having any. "I don't need protein," he bellowed. "I get enough from other places!" I assumed he meant the Jack Daniels. Then he went outside and passed out on the grass.

We ate for a long time and then went home loaded with leftovers. Just before we left, Mata found Rupert sitting on the toilet fast asleep. We were invited to return for New Year's Day.

Mata lived with Rupert and rented out her own house in Avatiu, but she and Kali seemed to live between both the houses; on Mondays, when Aiden and Tris were with her, they fed the pigs in Avatiu and went to Tupapa later in the afternoon. The boys hated Rupert, who seemed to have no kindness in him, and were always glad when he wasn't around. He seemed a strange choice of boyfriend for Mata, with her warm and generous heart. Maybe she felt sorry for him. Maybe no other woman on the island would have anything to do with him and she hated to see anyone alone. That's the only explanation I can come up with. But lord knows, the human heart is a perverse and tricky organ.

Friday, December 27

It is a lovely day—warm and windy. The ocean is rough (there's a storm up north) and the surf sounds very loud but the sun is out. I taught Aiden to play

127

chess last week and he has taken to it—he's setting up
the board so we can play a game before dinner. We sit
at the table in Emily's workroom, with its very tall
ceilings and its very tall French doors, palm trees just
outside and the light pearly and soft. All the doors are
open and sometimes a butterfly gets blown in. The
moko watch us from upside down on the ceiling.

We had started to see more and more of Fiona. She found
her way to our house one morning when Oskar and Alma,
who were going to school, missed the bus and she had to
drive them into town. She was working on a project making pinhole photographs using a camera she had made
herself from an enormous old biscuit tin. She had rented
a house near Kay George's gallery and was anxious to
spend as much time as possible away from it, given it was
owned by a large family of Jehovah's Witnesses who lived
on the upstairs floor and saw Fiona and her children as
ripe for the plucking.

Talking to Fiona was like drinking very nice champagne, a little yeasty with bubbles that tickle your nose.
Later, when we had got to know each other well, she
talked about it—about knowing she was like the bubbles
and her fear that perhaps she was *only* the bubbles. Seeing
as how she was so incandescent and pixie-like, no one
took her too seriously, including herself. She already
knew Ted and Tim and Nate, all of whom smiled at her,

enchanted, whenever she was talking and didn't hear a word she said. This made her worry, naturally, that she was meaningless. How different the world would be, though, if pompous blowhards were routinely ignored and everyone got giddy on champagne and found the courage to pursue their fantastical dreams. We would go off with enormous biscuit-tin cameras tucked under our arms and live in little pools of sunshine, no matter how hard it rained.

Jonathan called me sometimes in the evenings from his parents' house in New Jersey. We talked about feeling displaced. He disliked Switzerland, but he didn't feel at home back in the house where he had grown up. Home is one of those things, I suppose, that you can lose along the way. I wondered where my home was—back in the US somewhere? Sometimes it felt as though this island was my home, but I knew that it wasn't really. Maybe it just felt like home because Tris and Aiden were there. They were my home.

I don't remember how often I talked to Jonathan across the crackly overseas phone line. It was ruinously expensive for me to call him; he called me when he could. For the few weeks before he returned to Switzerland, he called me pretty often from his parents' house, letting them foot the bill, which I'm sure they loved, seeing they had always been rather horrified by me. Not that I blamed them. I had met them twenty years before, at the apex of my high-punk, bondage-gear, mini-skirted fabulousness. I remember them smiling in frozen mortification when they saw me. Their sweet-faced, well-behaved, cultured son—former captain of the math team, editorial editor of the high school paper, president of the RESISTORS— Radically Emphatic Students Interested in Science, Technology, and Other Research Subjects—had brought home a cross between Lizzie Borden and Hester Prynne. It is entirely possible that I licked Jon's face in front of them. Someday, one of my boys will bring home a de-frocked evangelical youth camp minister working as a part-time lobbyist for the National Rifle Association and Jonathan's parents will have their revenge.

Wild dogs roamed the island in packs, hunting by dawn among the roadside rubbish bins and the nests of the island chickens. Although I am not the sort who generally takes pleasure in the thought of baby chicks being devoured in their beds, my experiences with the wild roosters meant I wasn't entirely sure where—in the Darwinian struggle between the chickens and the dogs— my sympathies lay. In the end the matter was decided for me when Tris was chased, screaming in a high-pitched wail all the way across the garden, by a dive-bombing mother hen whose brood of babies he had stumbled across in the gardenia bushes. After that we gave a wide berth to nests or anything that looked like nests, and figured the chickens were more than able to take care of themselves.

Dogs, on the other hand, were a staple of the traditional Cook Islands diet—so much appreciated, in fact, that there is today not a single dog on the island of Aitutaki. As a consequence, the dogs on Rarotonga had a hunted, furtive look. They also looked mangy and worm-ridden and so were doubtless safer than they thought. After Christmas I broke down and started feeding a pack that came by the house in the mornings. I couldn't stand to see their ribs sticking out—especially one female, worn out from having puppies and giving me a look that said, "*You* understand." Even though Emily had been very strict about never feeding the dogs lest we were overrun by teeming hordes, I rummaged through the refrigerator while the dog waited patiently on the lawn. She wolfed down two chicken breasts, half a can of cat food and a large tub of marinated raw fish left over from Christmas.

Friday, January 3

The wild chickens are up to something today. So far I've seen five of them walking around on branches of the tipani trees and roosting in them. It's a strange sight. I didn't know chickens could fly.

Mata stopped by a couple of days ago to say that Emily is coming home tomorrow night, so tomorrow is our last day with the house all to ourselves. It's sunny

today and warm—no wind, very still and quiet. I can't
hear the ocean over the sound of the boys.

Emily had shown considerable trust leaving us all alone in charge of her house and all her worldly possessions while she was away for three months in New Zealand. It was my intention to show her that her trust had not been misplaced. That meant I had work to do.

First, I had to break the children of the habit of using the cushions off the furniture on the veranda as padding for the racecourse they had constructed across the front of the house. Then I went to the general store and bought a slip cover for the couch that Tris had used as a landing pad for various gymnastics, including shimmying up a support post to the rafters and then jumping straight down on to the couch—another fun game I had to end.

I also had to subtly coach the children not to *lie* exactly, but to at least imply we had been going to church *sometimes*. I took them to Sunday mass twice so that, when we started accompanying Emily every week again, the chance would be minimised of one of them piping up, "What's this place?" Hopefully they would show resigned inevitability, rather than shocked disbelief.

Then I had to disperse the hordes of dogs that had congregated in our front garden once the word got out about the leftover raw fish. And I had to hurry down to the Telecom office to pay the last month's phone bill in advance, feeling strange and shy about Emily knowing I had been calling some man on the other side of the world and talking to him late at night. After that I buzzed around for a couple of days sweeping and cleaning and straightening up the house.

My anxiety turned out to be completely unjustified: Emily was relieved to be back home and happy to see us. But then I blew it all by having a massive car wreck the next morning. In a way, I suppose, I had been waiting for this crash all my life, so much so that when it happened I wasn't the least bit surprised. It was a relief to finally have it over. There was an explosion, the earth careened, I felt a torrent of sharp edges and noise, and was aware of trying to spit out a mouthful of broken glass. I had never had broken glass in my mouth before. It was like straw, dry and prickly.

A maniac had hit us. The boys and I were in our car, waiting to turn right, and he was on a motorbike with his son on the passenger seat. He had zigzagged around all the cars, darting out into the traffic to the right of me just as I turned. He slammed into my door and the window exploded with the impact. He and his son were thrown off the bike into the road.

People stopped to help. The son's leg was broken and he was cut to the cheekbone. At first I thought the driver was in shock, but then it became clear that he was tremendously drunk. He stank of alcohol. The police arrived and took him and his son away to hospital in one car and drove us home in another. They were very kind, especially after the witnesses told them what had happened. Aiden looked up at me with round, scared eyes and said, "Are we going to prison now?" The policeman said, "No, no"— it was just an accident and we had done nothing wrong. I liked the way that Aiden asked if we were going "now" though. For him, it was apparently only a matter of time.

Neither he nor Tris were hurt at all. I was scratched, but nothing else—I didn't think I had actually swallowed any glass. I don't know if I was calmer now the crash had come and gone. I should have breathed easy that it wasn't worse, but I suspected it had only been the warning shot across my bow. The gods would get me yet. But not this time.

Meanwhile, the devout Mormon who owned the rental car agency assiduously cheated us by making us pay repair money for the car, looking me straight in the eye while telling bald-faced lies. The office girl had the decency to look away and blush furiously. I had a choice between fighting or letting the matter go. With a slight sigh of regret I chose the latter, testament to the subtle workings of the island on my psyche: it was much more pleasant just to pay up and go back to my shady spot under the palm trees.

Emily and I fell back into our routine of making 'eis in the morning and then sitting on the veranda whiling away the time. I was supposed to be working, and although I did sometimes spend an afternoon reading "books of value to my project", I still had months to go before my research had to be finished. It was much more interesting rummaging through Emily's memories. Our days were very serene, sitting on the porch, watching the boys climb trees or play together in the shade.

From the fascinating shelves of the Bounty Bookshop, Tris acquired a purple water balloon that he began taking care of—tenderly, as if it were his child. He called it "Precious Baby". Aiden started calling it "Precious Baby" too. For a while it lived in a dish on the bedside table, then in a little nest of cushions on a couch on the veranda. For a long time, it lived in the fruit bowl on the kitchen table. There were not a lot of toys available on the island. It didn't seem to matter very much.

By January it was incredibly hot—hardly a breath of breeze and no rain. It was hard to sleep at night. Fiona stopped by our house early one morning after driving her children to school. She was wearing only a pareu, the simple cotton wraparound used by locals as a skirt or dress. We sat on the veranda with Emily and talked. Fiona said the pareu was a problem: she was so flat-chested that when she tied it tight under her arms to keep it from slipping down, it cut off the circulation to her head.

I had decided that, having come this far across the South Pacific, it would be a shame if we did not go to Easter

Island. Now that Emily was back to handle the 'ei business, the boys and I set off for a couple of weeks, stopping first in Tahiti to wait for the twice-a-week plane and then continuing on to Easter Island, the south-eastern corner of the Polynesian triangle anchored by Hawai'i in the north and New Zealand in the south-west.

Easter Island, called Rapa Nui by Māori, is the most isolated inhabited place on Earth. Even the research stations on Antarctica have nearer neighbours than the people on Rapa Nui. The distance means that unlike, for example, Stonehenge, with its hordes and barriers and car parks and entrance fees, on Rapa Nui you can be alone with the massive stone heads, known as moai, that are scattered all over the island. We spent our first day strolling among some moai that stood on a raised stone platform at the edge of town.

"I don't think you should be up there," said Aiden, when I climbed up close to look at one.

When our guide the next day told us never to climb up on the platforms because they are also sacred burial sites, Aiden shot me a look and said loudly, "Told you."

I was accustomed, by that time, to the overlay of Britishness on Rarotonga—accustomed to saying "anticlockwise" rather than "counterclockwise", drinking innumerable cups of tea, and having bashful conversations with Nate Flynn—so it was something of a shock to find, on top of the indigenous Māori culture, a thick layer of

South American sexiness courtesy of the Chileans who seemed to run everything. Even the constant presence of my two boys didn't stop the waiter at the restaurant next to our hotel from effectively transcending the language barrier. What can be extremely irritating, even frightening, to pretty women in their twenties can be idly intriguing to those of us fast approaching Maggie May territory, or perhaps already deep in it. The waiter was attractive, witty and, as best I could tell, innocent in his attentions: he was flirting just because he was a flirt (although had I chosen to take him up on it ... well, there are worse ways to spend an afternoon).

Tuesday, January 21
Dear Jonathan,

> *The boys and I are on Easter Island for a little vacation. I wish you could be here with us. There is a wild and solitary beauty to everything. We are staying at a pensione looking down on the sea—very serene. Not too many tourists. Not too many cars—mostly horses that gallop fast along the edges of the faraway cliffs. Thinking of you as always.*
> *Love, Kathy*

When I got back to Rarotonga, I sent a long email to my friends back in the US.

Monday, February 3
Kia orana everyone,

Thought I'd keep you all up to date with the situation here in paradise. The Cook Islands government fell last week and the deposed politicians were immediately replaced by other politicians who are exactly like the first politicians. Comforting, in a way. Meanwhile, the Muslim Hippie Yoga Terrorists have left Samoa six months early under suspicious circumstances. Folasaitu Annandale—known as Joe to his friends, according to the article in the newspaper— is being tight-lipped, but apparently the group's leader has some sort of a God complex and one ex-member has accused them of being a cult. If I've said it once, I've said it a thousand times: "No good ever comes from yoga."

The boys and I have been doing some travelling. It was startling to realise how accustomed to Raro we've become. Tahiti, for instance, reduced us to the state of slack-jawed yokels. "Look, Mom," Aiden shrieked in the taxi from the airport, "a stop light!" Then he and Tris pressed their noses to the window, awed by the splendour of the changing colours. Besides traffic signals, Tahiti also has multistoried buildings, clean water, a seemingly endless supply of reliable electricity, and the world's prettiest prostitutes—all equally shocking to our provincial eyes. The island of

Tahiti itself has fifteen times the population of
Rarotonga, and Papeete, the capital, has exactly fifty
times the population of our capital "city" of Avarua. It
felt like being in downtown Manhattan or Hong Kong
compared to our sleepy world here in the shade of the
frangipani trees. People say that eighty years ago
Tahiti was like Rarotonga, and I can see it with the
steep misty mountains rising up in the centre and the
palms and hibiscus and wild gardenias. Our view of
Point Venus, where Captain Cook observed the transit
of Venus across the sun on his first Pacific voyage in
1769, was obscured by power lines and towering
cranes, and Matavai Bay was polluted and murky.
The restaurants were filled with disappointed tourists
searching for a place that no longer exists.

From Tahiti we went to Easter Island and
stepped into another world. It is part of Polynesia and,
despite being five time zones and 5000 kilometres from
Rarotonga, the indigenous language is similar to
Rarotongan. This is fortunate because Easter Island is
a territory of Chile and the official language is
Spanish, of which I know only the two phrases Alvis
taught me the night before my first trip to Guatemala:
"Where around here can a girl get a cold beer?" and
"Don't shoot me—I'm Catholic."

The island is lovely in a lonesome and time-
forgotten way. There is no protective coral reef so fierce

ocean waves pound against rocky cliffs; we saw the sun-bleached bones of something big at the base of one of them. The island is triangular with a volcano at each tip and high, windswept plateaus covered in eucalyptus, rosemary and herds of untamed horses in the centre. Late one afternoon we were standing in a sparse grove of palm trees at the edge of one of the only two beaches on the island—Anakena, where six of the stone statues sit with their backs to the water— when a herd of thirty or forty horses emerged over the crest of the hill behind us, galloped past, streamed through the statues in the sand, and disappeared over the hill on the other side. It was heartbreakingly beautiful.

There are only three thousand inhabitants and almost all live in the town of Hanga Roa, which is tranquil and pleasant, with a few paved streets (one in asphalt, the others in lovely zig-zag shaped bricks) and some gentle red-dirt roads that meander off into the countryside. People ride horses through the streets and build low stone walls around their gardens as protection from the wind. I fell momentarily in love with the proprietor of a small restaurant at the end of our street who flirted wickedly with me in Spanish.

"Wow," Aiden said to me, "you're sure learning this language fast."

I found myself thinking that I could live there

forever. Still, it was good to come back home to our
own ragged, cloud-hung mountains and our own
sunlit sea and even our own breadfruit trees. (I find
that I am starting to acquire a taste for breadfruit—I
just hope it's not a gateway food to sea cucumber and
Labrador retriever.) It's the height of summer and we
are drowsy and indolent. We sprawl on the veranda
reading or playing Parcheesi, and drinking the cold
juice of green coconuts through straws stuck through
the coconuts' eyes. Oh wait—working, that's what I
meant to say. We're all working very, very hard
indeed. I hope you are doing likewise.

Kia manuia, Kathy

While we were gone, Jonathan had called twice and a
small stack of letters from him had piled up on the table in
the hallway. Emily smiled knowingly while handing them
to me.

By now the difference between being a renter of a
room in the house and a member of the family had completely evaporated. Emily put us gently to work on a
major summertime house cleaning. As a start she had
decided to clean the finely woven straw mat, with its
beautiful pattern of leaves and flowers in faded green and
ivory, that covered the kitchen floor. Once we carried the
mat outside, shook it and left it to air on the veranda, we

realised that it had been concealing a trapdoor to a cellar. Aiden and Tris were fascinated—equally attracted and frightened by the spidery darkness below. Emily said that, as children, they had been afraid of what was under the house. Her father's whaling harpoon was, she said, stored down there. She didn't seem to be too eager to investigate. She hinted of ghosts. Frank, she said, had made fruit wine and stored it in the cellar. He had said the empty crawl space, and the floorboards expanding and contracting with changes in humidity and temperature, were what caused the strange sounds in the night. Emily and I agreed with each other—perhaps a bit too enthusiastically—that this was undoubtedly the case.

Emily said the crawl space extended beneath the whole house. It was to let the air in so as not to perish the floor. Emily spoke this sort of antique English. Everyone else said "petrol", for instance, but whenever Mata did a lot of driving for Emily, Emily would give her ten dollars "for the benzene". The boys had started to pick up some of Emily's phrases. "Rubbish!" they would say in her delicately enunciated way.

Emily wanted to get her computer fixed. It was an ancient thing given to her by Emona and had been broken for months and months, its insides corroded by salt air. There was supposed to be a guy in Matavera who could fix computers, so I drove her out one afternoon to try and find him. It was always an adventure to try and find something new because nothing on the island had an address. How could there be proper addresses when pathways meandered into the jungle and suddenly sprouted a couple of new houses, only one of the houses never got finished even though people sometimes lived there for a while, and then eventually the jungle took it back? Numbering the houses would be like numbering the seashells that appeared on the beach in the mornings and disappeared again overnight, so directions mostly referred as much to history as to geography. And "just past that field where Aunty Noo used to keep that spotted cow" was a good way to give directions because it also let you get in a good Aunty Noo story or two. You could fill a whole long summer afternoon just getting directions to the dentist.

Emily and I put the boys in the back seat and headed off towards Matavera. Emily knew where Matavera was of course, but I had only a vague idea, not because I had never been there—I had driven through hundreds of times—but because "Matavera" was a vague entity. The boundaries of all the villages on the island were hard to distinguish because one village flowed seamlessly into the next. Two hundred years ago the villages had been separate, each with its own sacred grounds, and there was no one living out in the surrounding jungle. That was the world by which Emily still navigated, and which was passed down from generation to generation.

I still had to look at the bus route map, but I was slowly starting to know the villages. When we drove along the road, I would say their names in my head as we passed through them, like a long esoteric poem:

Avarua (town)

Avatiu (where Mata has a house)

Panama (where we live)

Nikao (where the hospital road is)

Black Rock (where the souls of the dead depart for Ava'iki)

Arorangi (where the sun sets and Fiona lives)

Vaima'anga (where the abandoned hotel is)

Avaavaroa (where the road comes out of the forest at the edge of the bay)

Takitumu (where there is a rubbish bin painted with fish)

Titikaveka (where we swim)

Muri (where the sailing club is)

Ngatangi'ia (where the hidden harbour is)

Matavera (where the abandoned packing shed is)

Pue

O'oa

Tupapa (where Mata and Rupert live)

Avarua (again)

We found the computer guy eventually—by luck and Emily's memory, and because, frankly, there weren't that many houses. He turned out to be the son of a cousin and we had a nice long chat, first with him and then with his mother, who came out of another house hidden in the bush behind. He couldn't fix the computer. It didn't matter that much really, though, because Emily didn't know how to use the computer anyway.

We went back home the long way around the island, just for the drive. Ngatangi'ia, Muri, Titikaveka, Takitumu, Avaavaroa …

GHOSTS

I n the Cook Islands, land cannot be sold. It can be leased for ninety-nine years to outsiders, but it always ultimately belongs to the family. Hence, family lands go back centuries and centuries. Emily grew up in the house her grandfather had built, and that she expected her grandchildren would return to someday. It was a very different way of thinking about place than in America. Where my children will someday scatter my ashes, I have no idea. What should be done with me? This question would not bother us if we were Cook Islanders, for whom there is always the land that is home to return to.

Out behind Emily's house, like most other houses on the island, was the family graveyard. From Emily's kitchen window you could see two giant breadfruit trees, then a rambling clump of tiare māori bushes and beyond them the graves, glittering white in the sun. The ancestors rested there, although they were by no means quiet. They kept watch over the goings-on at the house, taking an extraordinarily active role in the daily life of the inhabitants. Johnny told me the ghosts at the library grumbled and muttered whenever the librarians worked late at night, and once let out an enormous, exasperated sigh of relief when she finally turned out the lights after an especially long evening. Of course, the sigh could have simply been the wind. Or creaky floorboards. Or overwrought imagination. Or a cat. There were many possibilities.

It seemed, though, that our house really was haunted. Just after Emily got back from New Zealand, Aiden said he saw someone glowing in our room at night. I told him it was just his imagination and there were no such things as ghosts. Then I saw it, next to my bed one night in February, glowing faintly green in the dark, the head of a man just at the height where a head would be if it were on a body, which this head, however, was not. It moved slowly through the room from the veranda door to the inside door that connected us to the rest of the house. It then passed through the closed door and disappeared.

The wardrobe stood just on the other side of that door. This was not inconsequential: the boys had been telling me for months that two little boys lived in the mirror of the wardrobe. They called to Aiden and Tris in soundless voices inviting them to come into the mirror. But Aiden said that the world beyond the mirror was a sad shadow world. He and Tris refused to go there. The little boys' names were Dick and John. I had not paid much attention to the game of Dick and John trapped in the wardrobe mirror—until Emily told me those were the names of her two dead brothers.

Emily and Frank had moved Emona's bed out of the room with the wardrobe when she was a little girl and no one ever slept there now, but it didn't feel as though the ghosts were malevolent. It was possible Emily's dead relatives just liked living in the house with us. Maybe they had become used to having us around and so didn't bother to be invisible any more.

It was not especially disturbing to live in a haunted house. It was rather friendly. On the walls of the hallway there were old heavy-framed pictures of some of the people resting under the white gravestones out back, which made it more convivial: it is comforting to have a clear idea of who is haunting you.

Fiona envied us our ghosts. Her house was quite new and the Jehovah's Witnesses had a mass cemetery behind the meeting hall in Takitumu, so she was pretty sure she wasn't being haunted. Emily and I looked askance at each other when she said things about wishing for ghosts at her house. Even though ours were friendly enough, Emily and I felt braver with each other around.

Sometime after Emily came back, we discovered we had inadvertently stolen someone's suitcase from the airport. It had been sitting in the middle of the floor for five months without our realising it. There was a time in my life when I would not have thought such a thing was possible.

It seemed that when Emona and her family had come to visit last September, on the way they had met Emona's son, Russell, in the airport in Auckland; he had flown there from Australia, where he lived with his father, Emona's first husband. The whole family had then continued on to Rarotonga and at two in the morning Mata had picked them up at the airport. When they were loading their suitcases into Mata's truck, they had apparently picked up an extra one by mistake. It must have been sitting on the floor close to their luggage, and either Arthur, Emona's husband, had put it in the truck thinking it was Russell's, or Russell had put it in the truck thinking it was Arthur's or Emona's. Of course, they wouldn't necessarily recognise each other's luggage. And, of course, the arrival area would, as always, be pandemonium.

When they got to our house in the middle of the night, Arthur had put the suitcase in the middle of the floor in the bedroom where Russell was going to sleep, thinking it must be Russell's. Now, in many houses someone might notice a gigantic brown suitcase sitting unopened for two weeks in the middle of their bedroom floor. Not in ours. Russell was sleeping in the inside bedroom—the one with the haunted wardrobe and the open closet all along one wall crammed with old dresses—so he probably just thought it was part of Emily's stuff, along with all the other clothes and boxes and bundles and Christmas ornaments and bug-eaten board games and embroidered table linens and mismatched shoes piled around. And when they all went back to New Zealand, taking Emily with them, it was left behind. Nobody missed it because it wasn't theirs. And I ignored it for three months for the same reason that Russell did.

Emily noticed it when she came back in January, but she thought it was mine. I found this out when she asked me one day if I would move it. After a Laurel and Hardy half-hour when I kept trying to put it in her bedroom and she kept trying to put it in mine, the truth dawned, so we carried it into the work room and cracked it open. It contained some miscellaneous ugly-but-serviceable-for-travelling clothes—wrinkle-free polyester with loud, busy patterns that meant the dirt wouldn't show.

There were also two books in a possibly Scandinavian language. "It's French?" Emily said. "Not French, I think," I said. Aiden and Tris each had a long hard look in case they might recognise it. They didn't. "But it's not French, that's for sure," Tris said, with conviction born of mastering almost the entire alphabet (upper- and lower-case) except for Q, W and sometimes Y. There was also a slip of paper taped inside with a name and a telephone number, but no address.

It was immediately obvious to Emily that international phone calls to possibly Scandinavian countries in order to explain how five months ago we had inadvertently stolen a piece of someone's luggage would fall under my department. First came the part where I figured out how many noughts and ones to add to the beginning of the telephone number in order to get the right international access line. I finally got it figured by dialling every possible three-digit and four-digit combination of nought and one until I eventually hit the right one.

Then there was the part where I got fast buzzes or slow buzzes or bewildering beeping noises. Then came the part where I got an answering machine speaking a language very definitely not French. There was a long silence after the beep during which I imagined explaining to the owners of the suitcase how it had all happened, and to the officials at the airport and possibly to Customs and Air New Zealand that I would like them to send the suitcases back to not France but somewhere else without charging us. I was pretty certain that returning inadvertently stolen property would also fall under my department since my department had radically expanded in the months since Emily's return to cover everything that involved (one) filling out forms, (two) making repeated trips to inexplicably closed offices, and (three) paying fees, so inside my head I thought, "Welcome to Polynesia" and hung up on the answering machine without saying anything at all.

"Well?" Emily asked. "No one there," I said and shrugged helplessly.

We repacked the suitcase and shoved it under the bed in the haunted bedroom so it would be there if anyone came looking for it. I have no doubt it is there still.

There were four bedrooms in Emily's house, and two bathrooms, a big one in the main part of the house and a small one off our bedroom at the front of the house. Once Aiden, Tris and I moved into this bedroom, Emily returned to the big bedroom at the back where the boys and I had slept when we first moved in. There was another small bedroom where Emily had slept for a while and where I had spent many mornings sitting on the floor making 'eis when Emily first hurt her back, and there was the large seldom-used bedroom where Russell had slept. Besides the haunted wardrobe, this bedroom also had the open closet with dozens of Emily's old dresses—gorgeous dresses made of silk in delicate shades of ivory, copper and sage, all with faded tags in the back saying "Empire Made".

Around late November, with Emily safely in New Zealand, I worked up the courage to start trying them on. Emily was by then a little smaller than I was, bent and shrunken with age, but sixty years earlier when the dresses had been made we must have been the same size. They fitted me perfectly; I looked as though I should be served tea after a game of croquet. It was lovely to walk through the house in the dresses, feeling the cool silk flowing around my bare legs. Emily must have looked beautiful in them when she was young, with her golden skin and long black hair. It occurred to me to steal one of the dresses, but mindful of the ever-watchful ghosts I put them all back very carefully before Emily returned.

My own clothes had been brought with an eye towards South Seas romance rather than practicality. I hadn't been able to stand the thought of a whole year in wrinkle-free polyester. Instead, I had brought just two dresses, one in blue and green cotton and one in rose-coloured linen that had been slowly fading to an ever paler pink as it was worn relentlessly, washed numerous times in Emily's ancient washing machine and hung in the bright sunshine to dry. The linen was not constructed to hide its wrinkles and, ironing being a laughable proposition in that heat, I usually looked rather more crumpled than specifically romantic.

The truth was, none of us had very elegant clothes. Emily wore the same four or five cotton print dresses week after week. Fiona had a pale blue skirt she wore every-where, and a pair of bright red cotton trousers for special occasions. Nate Flynn almost always wore the same pair of worn khaki shorts and scuffed leather sandals. There was, though, a woman named Kara, whom I got to know later, who showed up at art gallery openings in a leopard-print dress and high heels with rhinestones.

By February, I was getting a letter every three or four days from Jonathan. Now that Emily was back, she checked our mailbox in town most days. She smiled at me a lot when she handed over the letters.

Jonathan mailed his letters in envelopes from his office, so they had a big blue "IBM" printed on the outside. When we reached the stage of teasing each other about the frequency of our communications, he asked me if Emily found it strange that I was getting so many letters from IBM.

"Does she think a computer salesman is trying psychotically hard to get you to purchase a new laptop?"

I laughed of course, because Emily had never in a million years heard of IBM—or even of laptops. Besides, she knew exactly what was going on, long before even I did.

Sometimes when Mata was looking after the boys, instead of doing interviews or copying down government statistics for my research I would sneak to the Telecom office at the edge of town and call Jonathan from the long-distance booth. It was two o'clock in the morning for him, but he said he didn't mind. I just wanted to hear his voice. He has a very deep voice, like a bear that's been eating warm honey.

Fiona had now met all the artists on the island and charmed them with her vivacious exuberance. Ted, especially, was smitten and became very gentle and endearing whenever he was around her. This was in stark contrast to the solemn Māori warrior persona he had around me.

However, Fiona, it turned out, had a long-distance boyfriend back in England and paid some shocking fee for a computer connection to be installed in her house so she could email him every day. She was somewhat torn about having a boyfriend, feeling that being on her own was empowering and freeing and beautiful, and that a woman certainly didn't need to be always hooked to some man. On the other hand, men were so enticing—at least the good ones—smart and sexy and nice-smelling. Who could resist? Fiona's boyfriend had a crooked smile and an exceedingly dry wit. She had been doomed from the moment she met him.

Meanwhile her daughter Alma, who was fourteen and even more attractive than her mother, was having some problems with jealousy from the other girls at her school. There had been name-calling and an unpleasant incident in the hallway. Fiona was having a ticklish time trying to explain to Alma the reason for the girls' hostility. "I told her," said Fiona, "that the women in our family have always been very, very generous." Emily nodded wisely (we were all sitting together on the veranda).

*

In early February, Hurricane Dovi passed by just west of the island. There was a lot of rain and wind, but no flooding or damage. It was actually sort of nice sitting around on the veranda watching the chickens get wet and listening to the weather reports on the radio. Unfortunately, though, when the rain stopped it left sweltering heat in its wake. The ground that had been saturated with water for a week steamed in the heat of the sun. The humidity was so intense that even reading made us sweat, and the only comfortable place to be was floating half-submerged in the lagoon. As I was reading a lot it was hard to clear my mind when someone tried to talk to me. The boys, meanwhile, were hardly ever away from me. They talked to me continually, no matter what I was doing. They migrated along behind me wherever I went—from our room to the veranda to the kitchen to the bathroom to the garden and back to the veranda.

I bought an ancient hand-held slide viewer for two dollars at the library. The library was privately run and supported itself through donations, used book sales and an occasional rummage sale like this one, where people dug fantastic things out of their attics and then bought other people's equally fantastic things for fifty cents or a dollar.

In the box that came with the viewer there were a bunch of slides. Two little boys stood next to an American car holding Easter baskets. The same two boys dug a hole in a yard with shovels. Flowers bloomed in hanging porch pots. A woman held a kitten in front of some luxuriant rose bushes. This slide was labelled: "Mrs J.V. Patton, Otter Rock, Oregon, Sept 1950". A smiling man genially held up a fish. This one said: "Mr Frank Watson, Otter Rock, Oregon, Sept 1950—12 lb. fish". There were also some slides labelled "El Paso Christmas Lights", which seemed to have been taken around the same time.

The box said "Zadiix 35mm Slide Strip Viewer— Royal De-Luxe—A QUALITY VIEWER with Clear Undistorted Magnification, Natural Life-Like Effect".

I wasn't too impressed with the Natural Life-Like Effect: the colors seemed oddly orange. But the view did seem Clear and Undistorted, in a hard-edged way that was surreal in its sharpness. Mr Frank Watson was somehow more clear and undistorted than any of the real people standing near me in the library garden.

Malcolm told me one day when we were still living in his motel that he needed his glasses only when he was on land; when he was out at sea on his vaka his eyesight was clear and sharp. Now I understood what he meant. A hazy glow of sunlight on the island made people look a little blurry around the edges. In fact everything had a halo of sultry light. Māori called Rarotonga Te Enua Ou Tumu Te Varovaro—The Misty Land Whence Comes the Thunder—so perhaps they knew that from the beginning.

Frank Watson looked quite strange: it had been a long

time since I had seen anything in another light. I wondered how the slides had come to be there, mouldering on the lawn in the library rummage sale. A sticker on the box said "Shipped to Rarotonga Courtesy of AIR NEW ZEALAND", but most library books had that stamped on them so it didn't explain much. Maybe objects migrated to the island through a series of downward steps—from living rooms to attics to yard sales to Salvation Army collections, and then, when someone got tired of them taking up shelf space at a thrift shop, to the island. Whatever the case, the slide viewer had taken fifty years to work its way here. We were a long way from Otter Rock, Oregon.

Meanwhile, the ancestors were certainly busy earning their sacrificial virgins. One day in mid February, while I was at Dr Tamarua's getting Aiden diagnosed with mumps for the second time, Emily rented out the unused bedroom to two foreigners that Mata was throwing out of her house in Avatiu because they were filthy, unpleasant, and very late with the rent.

This did not seem a great recommendation for having these people come to live with us. Nevertheless, they arrived that night and moved in. Emily wanted to give them the back bedroom, which was large and light-filled and didn't block the entrance to the laundry room, but they insisted on having the inside room, a strange choice because the room had no windows or outside doors and was piled full of Emily's old clothes, stacked to the ceiling in sagging brown cardboard boxes and hanging in the closet and the old wardrobe (which was, of course, haunted).

The couple was from Romania. And the woman's name was Romania. We think. In any case, Mata called her Romania and she responded positively. Well, we think she responded positively but we were not absolutely sure of this because she spoke only Romanian and none of us spoke Romanian at all. For all we knew, she was telling Mata to stop calling her Romania or else.

Romania (Emily called her "the woman") was in charge. Her husband, who apparently had no name—or if he did it didn't matter—was emphatically *not* in charge. They both had very white skin and the woman was wearing dark sunglasses even though it was night when they arrived. "Hey, Romania!" Mata said, "Why are you wearing your sunglasses at night?" Romania didn't answer. She just went straight into her new bedroom, closed the door and locked it very loudly. This was a little odd because the bedroom had another entrance with no door that led to the laundry room. But we got the point.

Later, her husband came out and made her some tomato soup and disappeared back into the bedroom without cleaning up the kitchen. Then he nailed a blanket over the open doorway between their bedroom and the laundry room. It must have been stifling in there. Emily was really angry about having to clean up the mess from the soup. The man, who spoke English, told us later that he was going to clean it up eventually, but that Emily had got to it first.

My theory was that they were vampires and therefore couldn't go out in the sunlight, and that the tomato soup was really warmed up blood. At first, Mata didn't give this much credence, but she slowly came around to my point of view. Emily and the boys were on board from the start.

It transpired that the Romanians were running a hotel in Arorangi. Most people who run hotels live in them, but they said they wanted somewhere to go during the day so the hotel guests couldn't bother them. They said—that is, the man told Mata and Mata told Emily and me—that we should all be quiet during the day so we didn't disturb them. (I pointed out later that, being vampires, they would of course need to sleep all day.) The man said they had to stay out of the sun because Romania was allergic to sunlight. It struck Mata and Emily and me that running a hotel on a tropical island might not be the best career choice for a sun-allergic misanthrope.

In the morning the man made Romania another bowl of blood, which she drank in seclusion in the bedroom, and then they departed, leaving another mess in the kitchen. At the time I was wrestling antibiotics down Aiden's throat. He put up a good fight, involving lots of screaming and defensive tongue action, but I prevailed. The swelling went down considerably.

We never saw Romania again. The man found Mata in town and told her they couldn't handle Emily getting mad at them for the mess in the kitchen. Then he came to the house to retrieve their luggage and told Emily that Aiden and Tris were too noisy. But Mata and Emily and I knew the truth: the ghosts in the wardrobe had chased them away. Emily thought the ancestors had come to Aiden in the morning and made him misbehave when he was taking his medicine. "He's never like that usually," she said, as evidence for her case. (This was not strictly true, but I decided to let it go.)

I myself imagined that it was more of a frontal assault issuing directly from the wardrobe itself. "After all," I told Emily, "I wouldn't sleep in there."

Emily looked at me sideways and repeated what Frank had told her: "If you want to see a ghost badly enough, you will." But she didn't ever sleep in the room. Anyway, they were gone and we were glad.

A couple of days later there was a front-page story in the newspaper saying the couple were being removed from running the hotel and possibly deported. The hotel had been cited for seventeen major violations of health and safety codes. Complaints from guests were piling up at the tourism office. We had unwittingly provided a hide-out for them from the authorities while they were on the lam; they had finally been tracked down as they fled from our wardrobe. The couple was fighting the deportation. The story reported them as saying that the tourists were a bunch of whiny crybabies who didn't even know how to unstop a clogged toilet or put out a small electrical fire by themselves. They were identified in the story as "Romania" and "her husband".

Mata, Emily and I now all said we had known they were bad news from the start, and Mata and Emily each took me aside to tell me it was all the idea of the other one to get mixed up with them in the first place. Mata was working on getting them set up with a room at Emily's sister's house. I didn't even ask.

It was hard to learn to speak Māori, and in fact I never learnt more than a few phrases and words. Emily and Mata switched effortlessly between Māori and English. They spoke Māori to each other, but changed to English whenever I was in earshot. All of Emily's friends who came to visit were the same way. It would have been dreadfully rude, by Cook Islands standards, to speak a language in front of me that I didn't understand, so it was surprisingly hard for me even to hear Māori spoken.

In our long mornings on the veranda, I would ask Emily vocabulary words and how to say certain things. She would explain all the nuances, such as the different words for love. "Aipo" was the word for someone you love, but in a way that is both spiritual and sexual. You would never say it to your child. "How would I tell my children I love them?" I asked. Emily thought for a while to make sure she got it just right. "Akaperepere au ia korua" means "I love you both" with a type of "love" that means "cherish". "You cherish them," Emily said to me, watching them race through the garden in the sunlight, "e mate ua ata au—until I die." The words are written in her fine, spidery handwriting in my journal.

One night in late February Jonathan called and we talked for a long time. I pulled Emily's phone by its lengthy cord until I was out on the veranda and then sat in one of the deep armchairs, trying to pay attention to what he was saying while Aiden and Tris rampaged around me, bouncing a ball against the wall by my head and shrieking out commentary on whatever game they had made up.

Jon seemed to have a lot on his mind. He said, "I've been doing a lot of thinking," but then Mata arrived with Kali, and Tris wanted to sit on my lap, and Mata and Emily both asked me a series of very important questions ("Do you know anyone who is going to Aitutaki soon who could bring us back some mangoes?" "Have you seen the cat lately?" "What does Kay George do with the oysters that she gets at the market?"). So in between telling Jonathan that I was sure things would work out and not to worry about work until he got better and that he should pay attention to his doctor and get more sleep,

I was also saying, "Elise is" and "Yes, she was hunting mice in the bushes behind the house this morning. She eats them raw" and "If you're going to sit here, you have to stop kicking me." After about a half hour of this, Jonathan finally blurted out, "I'm trying to tell you that I *love* you!" Then, "I'm sorry. I wasn't going to tell you that." He was so terribly apologetic it made me laugh. "It's okay," I said at last, "I love you too", which caused absolute silence on the porch for the first time all day.

Emily began smiling slyly at me after that. "Your friend has a very nice voice," she said to me in an encouraging sort of way. (She was the one who had answered the phone.) "He seems like a very *nice* young man."

So I was in love. You have already figured out that I had been all along.

I realise this seems insane. Most of my contact with Jonathan for months had been by letter. How can you fall in love with someone by correspondence? It's not exactly like learning accounting in your spare time, after all. It is far more likely that I was merely delusional, swept away, at last, by the overpowering romanticism of the South Seas. Six months of palm trees and sunsets, the sonorous sound of the waves, the hot, sleepless nights, playing look-but-don't-touch with Nate Flynn: it would have taken a cooler heart and head than mine to remain untouched.

If it were magical for Jonathan and I to fall in love from half a world apart, what purpose would it serve to question too closely whether or not it was also sane? In the first flush of love, after all, who is sane? Maybe every love story is a little crazy.

And it was entirely appropriate that Jonathan and I should have made our declarations of love in the midst of so much commotion. In Polynesia, love is never just about two people alone: it is about all their families, all their friends and neighbours, and all the ghosts who roam around invisible among us. On a little island, love is about everyone because it touches everyone with its consequences.

After all those months of knowing him, I finally interviewed Nate Flynn for my book. He invited me to his house for lunch. His house was small, set back from the road and almost buried in hibiscus bushes. His paintings glimmered on the walls.

When I arrived, he was in the minuscule kitchen, cooking and drinking beers with a guy called Chuck. Chuck and I moved a table into the shade of a huge flame tree in the back garden. Nate's wife, who was very beautiful with a long graceful neck and a small neat head, arrived home with their kids just as we were sitting down. She took Nate's beer for herself and glared at me haughtily. She had obviously not been expecting me and was not at all appeased when I explained why I was there. "Oh, yes," she sneered, "Nate is a *great* artist. You people"—including Chuck in her contempt—"are all so keen on Nate. Nate, Nate, Nate! When are you going to go mad over *my* paintings?"

Chuck leaned drunkenly forward. "Maybe when you paint some," he hissed. Then he got up and swayed away, lurching through the hedge at the far end of the garden.

"Piss off," she said, either to him or me, I wasn't sure. Then she got up and stalked back into the house.

"Now then." Nate smiled at me, with just a flicker of irony behind his eyes. "What do you want to know?" The kids were unconcernedly eating their lunches so I opened myself a beer and started the interview.

Having fallen in love with Jonathan, I pretty much gave up Nate. This was relatively untraumatic, given I had never had him in the first place. Nevertheless, as Emily Dickinson said: "To lose what we / never owned / might seem an / eccentric Bereavement / but Presumption / has its Affliction / as actually as / Claim ..."

Like any place in the tropics, Rarotonga has mosquitoes. Tris and I were never bitten because we were always with Aiden, and the mosquitoes had such a decided preference for Aiden they just ignored everyone else. I told Aiden he must be especially sweet. It was small comfort: his legs looked like a war zone.

It wasn't too bad in the house because there were screens on the windows, and although the doors stood open all day long we closed them in the evenings, which helped. But we mostly spent our time on the veranda, which was, of course, completely open. We bought Fish

Brand mosquito coils, because of all the different brands the Fish Brand package was the prettiest. The coils were a Class IV Poison, but there had recently been a couple of cases of dengue fever, which could be fatal for young children and for which there was no vaccine and no cure, so it was the devil or the deep blue sea.

I kept mosquito coils burning whenever the weather was damp, and it was damp every day. This was part of the reason the elderly Polynesian women were so beautiful— their skin stayed moist and soft forever. It was impossible to have dry skin. It was also impossible to have dry matches. I tried to light the mosquito coils with wooden matches, but the tips of the matches were so saturated with water from the air they crumbled into soggy bits when I tried to strike them. The matchboxes came from the store wrapped in cellophane, and the matches were usable for about five days after the cellophane was removed, before they got too damp. I bought matchboxes by the dozens.

Kara, Lee and Ella came by our house one day when we were sitting on the veranda. Kara scrunched up her face disdainfully at the mosquito coils but Lee just laughed. "I grew up with those things. Whatever diseases they give you, I've already got 'em all," he said cheerfully.

I had met Kara and Lee through Fiona, who had met them through Kay George. Lee was from Malaysia and Kara was from Italy. Their daughter, Ella, was three years old and striking, with dark skin and green eyes.

Lee was an economic counsellor in the Cook Islands government, fighting against injustice and inequality, and one of the nicest, smartest men I knew. Kara, meanwhile, was playing at being a painter. She was very pretty and seemed to feel that in being pretty she had done all she needed to do. Nevertheless, we were friends—drawn together by the magnet that was Fiona. I was finding that I had somehow acquired a whole circle of friends. I now took the boys and Emily with me to art openings and birthday parties and invited lunches. For Emily it seemed almost as though, after years of quiet seclusion, the old times had come back, the days when she and Frank had parties on the veranda and she played the piano and everyone sang.

Emily got a big order to make the staff uniforms for a new restaurant that was opening up on the other side of the island. They were going to be royal blue trousers and shirts, with gold tiki silk-screened on them. A young woman from the restaurant would arrive each morning with cut pieces of fabric and Emily would silk-screen glittery gold paint around the cuffs of the trousers, and the collars and hems of the shirts. The woman would then pick up the painted pieces and take them back to be sewn up.

This was supposed to go on for a week, but it ended up taking much longer because Emily had to redo a whole bunch. She had mixed up the top and bottom of the trouser pieces and inadvertently outlined all the crotches in bright gold paint. When the pieces had been sewn together, little golden idols with spears were cavorting madly all around the waiters' flies, which was a striking effect but not exactly what the restaurant had in mind.

The owner was very upset and spoke sternly to Emily about the waste of cloth and added expense, blah blah blah. I didn't see what the problem was: the trousers were almost certainly highlighting the best thing about the restaurant.

While she was at it, Emily made hip little bowling shirts for the boys and a dress for me—ivory with designs silk-screened in light brown. We would have been *au courant* in the 1950s. All this added to my sense that I didn't know what year it was any more, or even what decade. Time on the island was not a straight arrow—it was bent and curved, the way Einstein described space as being. Things that had happened half a century earlier seemed nearer than things that had happened last year. The childhood of Emily's daughters, as related in Emily's stories, seemed to be happening at the same time as that of Aiden and Tris. The boys' voices echoed the voices of children who had played in this garden decades before. Our lives back in the United States now seemed so distant as to be imaginary.

Fiona was trying to set up an exhibition of her work. Ever since she arrived she had been photographing people with her biscuit-tin pinhole camera and printing the pictures in a makeshift darkroom she had slapped together in her bathroom. She spent hours squatting on the cramped floor of the sealed, light-tight room in the stifling heat with her nose just at the level of the toilet bowl (a toilet that was used, let's not forget, by her son, a twelve-year-old boy with somewhat indifferent aim). Whenever Kara complained that she couldn't possibly get any painting done because the working conditions on the island were too primitive, Kay George and I would look at each other silently and think of Fiona on the bathroom floor, trying not to drip sweat on to her wet negatives. And her photographs were beautiful.

When she knew us well enough, Fiona photographed Emily. She brought a lovely 'ei katu—a crown of gardenias, baby's breath, and ti leaves—for Emily to wear on her head, and set her up in a lovely beam of light coming through the skylight into the workroom. Then she carefully explained that Emily would have to sit perfectly still for three minutes because it was a very long exposure. Emily sat still for about ten seconds and then started scratching her head quite vigorously—the 'ei katu was tickly. "Ab-so-lute-ly still," Fiona reminded her, hoping the negative could still be saved. "Yes, yes," Emily said reassuringly. Then after another ten seconds, she had another violent scratching bout. And another. And another.

Fiona stopped by later with the negative—Emily had come out as a flowery blur.

*

Friday, February 21

Emily's brother, Akapi Akapi, died last night. We got the phone call early this morning. The grave is being dug in the family plot in the backyard right now. According to Cook Islands custom, the body has to be buried within a day. Mata is raking leaves to make the yard nice for all the people who will be here for the burial. I'm lurking around in our room. In line with traditional custom, we seem to have added a few new members to the household—relatives who may stay for days or months or years.

Sunday, February 23

Emily wanted us to come with her to Akapi's funeral. When we got to the church everyone was sitting solemnly outside under the trees. The casket was draped in a fine tivaevae quilt. After a while, it was carried inside and we followed. I didn't understand much of the funeral service, but Emily kept whispering translations to me. Then the singing began, with intense, cutting beauty. The older women, especially, sing a high, keening harmony that reaches back through a thousand years of time to some primitive wail of anguish and longing and grief. The whole building fairly trembled with it. I had never really heard Emily sing before; her voice was surprisingly harsh but lovely.

After the service there was food in an adjoining room, the table laden and people gorging themselves. I sat next to Mata and ate taro and chicken while she polished off about twenty corned beef sandwiches. People kept telling me to eat more: I am too skinny by Polynesian standards. I am very fond of Polynesian standards ...

After this everyone went to our house, where there was more food and where the fresh grave was waiting out in the backyard next to Emily's parents and Frank and her sister Nani's husband. The casket was lowered into the grave with the tivaevae still covering it and the grave was then filled with dirt. Later some men came to put a concrete vault on top.

After the funeral, most of the relatives left except for Emily's cousin Lena, who will live with us for a while. She is a widow but much younger than Emily— her husband died young. She seems very good-natured and works as a housekeeper for the prime minister. Lena, Mata, Emily and I sat together on the veranda after dinner (leftovers from the funeral) and talked while Aiden, Tris and Kali played in the garden. Emily was upset: someone at the funeral had said Akapi was lonely the last few years. No one should be lonely, she said. It is almost inconceivable for Emily's generation that people would ever be alone, much less lonely. It is completely incomprehensible that someone would actually seek out aloneness. She reached out and patted my arm, glad that we have each other. At dusk we all walked out to the graves. There is room for Emily, right next to Frank.

BELONGING

I t had been a long time since Emily's daughters had left, sailing away on the boat to the new world in New Zealand. During all those years, especially since Frank died, Emily had taken in boarders, fitful tenants who used the beds and the kitchen for a few weeks or months before moving on. Emily was not pushy and mostly let them be. I never once heard her mention any of them by name. She hadn't expected anything different from us either at first. The boarders paid her rent money that she didn't really need—she sent it on to her grandchildren—but the sounds they made in their rooms at night kept the old house from being so lonesome. That was all.

In the afternoons, the boys and Emily and I often went

for a drive on the back road. Emily had many friends along the way and we would stop by the side of the road whenever we saw one standing outside in her garden. Emily would chat merrily, leaning out the car window, while her friend would lean on a rake, or a fence, or the side of our car. Emily would always carefully introduce us, and her friend would smile and nod and file us away in the mental flow chart of relationships that every Cook Islander builds inside his or her head to keep the world in order.

I learnt that in Polynesia it is important to be able to recite your genealogy. People ritually do it, for example, at the beginning of important occasions when they are asked to speak. There was no written language in the Cooks until the missionaries came, so the past was kept as oral history, long stories of the ancestors memorised and repeated, over and over again. Emily could recite her genealogy going back generation after generation; she kept in her head a dense web of relationships that tied her to a huge network of living Rarotongans. These were all family and came to visit us whenever we didn't go to visit them. There was Rosa, who worked at the bank, and Mere, who worked at the CITC, and Marlene and Nga and Jake. And then there were the very old friends, such as Dolly and Mereanna, and Greta from the Philatelic Bureau. They all knew each other's stories.

The boys and I were now part of this web, with connections and ties that wove us tightly into the life of the island. I was aware, at the periphery of my senses, that we travelled under Emily's protection and that people whom we didn't know nevertheless knew us and knew that we belonged to her.

One day there was a story in the *Cook Islands News*: "Nauru cut off from rest of world since January." Nauru, an island north-west of Rarotonga, had apparently lost all telephone communication; diplomatic missions accredited to the island said they were not even certain any more who was president. "Already on the verge of bankruptcy," the story said, "Nauru has, for the past year or more, operated on just one international telephone circuit. But now the system has collapsed and Nauru has no money to fix it."

When I first read the headline, I found this intriguing. How lovely to be cut off from the rest of the world. How restful. I had visions of Shangri-La. But when the story went on to say that the electrical grid may also have failed and fuel was running short, I began to think about things such as medical care. How were they taking care of sick children? The country's leaders must have been madmen to have plunged their nation into this isolation. Isolation is lovely when you choose it for yourself, but my vision of perfect isolation involved sitting with Emily on the veranda, talking through the morning, and maybe having Mata come by, or Fiona. I would get letters from my Dad and Jonathan, and a fresh shipment of books would arrive at Bounty Bookshop to sift through. When I first came to the island, I had just wanted to be left alone with my little boys. Things had changed.

Around the time that Lena came to stay with us, Emily moved into the back bedroom, the one the boys and I had lived in at the beginning. Lena was using the little bedroom on the east side of the house where Emily had been sleeping. When Mata brought Aiden and Tris back one Monday afternoon, Rosa was visiting, and Emily asked if we would change around some mattresses for her. She wanted to move the mattress from the four-poster bed in the haunted bedroom on to her bed, and vice versa. The mattress on her bed was heavy—stuffed with kapok, I think—and unwieldy. The three of us wrestled its sagging, ponderous bulk through the doorway and tried to heave it up on to the four-poster bed, panting and laughing: we seemed like three ants with an enormous noodle. At one point I was trapped under a corner of the mattress, struggling and pushing with all my might, while Mata bent double with guffaws. Rosa laughed at me: "You're a real Cook Islands girl now."

Cook Islanders say that once you have smelled tiare māori—the wild gardenia—you will always come back to the island. You won't be able to resist. And when Emily and Frank started their silk-screened shirt business, it was the image of the tiare their homesick customers in New Zealand yearned for.

For me, the scent of the tiare was only one part of the overpowering perfume of the island for which I still long, even now. There were other things too: the smell of smoke on the early morning breeze; the ocean, of course; the gritty sawdust bitterness of the aisles of the CITC, and the acrid hot oil of the fried chicken takeaways. But more than anything else, it was the smell of the earth after the hard rain, when the sun came out and the green chlorophyll fecundity of vine, bush and creeper exploded in the heavy air.

With the sap and pollen and green leaves thick around me, it took no great stretch of the imagination to see Aiden and Tris as green and tender and luscious.

As for me, who am I to judge? Such evaluations are better left to others. But I do know that I was happy to wake up at dawn, happy to see the roosters and the hens and chicks, happy to see Emily and Mata and Fiona and Nate, happy walking through town to buy a newspaper in the clean morning air, with the ocean on one side and the lapis sky raised over me like an airy cathedral.

Wednesday, February 26

I have discovered starfruit growing on a tree in our backyard, and yesterday Emily picked a custard apple from a tree she thought had stopped producing. So in our yard we have: avocados, coconuts, pawpaws, guavas, Tahitian pineapples, limes, Malaysian pears,

179

passionfruit, starfruit, custard apples, green peppers,
and berries the name of which I don't know. Some of
the flowers are: seven types of tipani, tiare māori,
flame trees, six varieties of hibiscus, roses, morning
glory, big pink lilies, another flame-like flower that
looks like a tiny birdcage, beach hibiscus, and some
sort of golden flower that hangs down in long strands
from the trees like wisteria.

I got a letter from Jonathan mailed just two and
half weeks ago, a new postal speed record. Usually,
letters take about a month to arrive. I'm not sure how
it is possible for them to take so long. What could they
be doing? There is a classified ad in the paper this week
that says a boat for the outer islands will be leaving
next Wednesday, or maybe next Thursday or Friday—
depending on when they get around to loading it up.
No hurry. So I have a pretty good idea about where the
slow-down with the mail may be occurring.

It's a wonderful day today. The breeze comes
from the sea in waves that lift the branches of the
guava trees in a gentle arc before they fall slowly back
under the weight of ripe gold. They are like a slow
motion Marilyn Monroe of green and yellow—or like a
girl letting an ocean wind dry her hair.

For my high-school graduation my parents gave me a
single-lens reflex camera, and over the years it had become

almost a part of me. There had been times when I was more or less serious about being an artist, and although in the end I had chosen another career the urge to create, to make something, had remained irresistible. On this island where I spent my days—or at least my Mondays—talking with artists and seeing their studios, and where, so far from the beaten path, so distant from the limelight, where the art world still had the antic quality of kids deciding to put on a show in a barn, I found myself making art again. These were not just photos but also drawings and small watercolour paintings made with Tris's paint set. I even wrote the occasional extremely bad poem. Whenever Emily caught me at it, she would invariably recite for me a poem she had learned by heart as a schoolgirl. It began, "Oh Rarotonga, my lovely island home".

It was better for me to stick with photographs. I tried to make them look like scientific illustrations from the nineteenth century, botanical drawings with front views and side views and cross-sections and all the classifications written out in Latin and a ruler laid alongside to give a sense of scale. Unfortunately, however, my imagined Victorian photographer had stood too far back and accidentally included, on the edges of the frame, the surrounding flotsam and incidental jetsam. Those seemingly incidental things are really what the photographs are about—a scattering of the things that made up our lives: old library books and empty bottles, half-eaten guavas, feathers and flowers and shells, and dead cockroaches lying on their backs.

I wanted to make a photograph for Jonathan like that—a picture ostensibly of a sprouted coconut. For the labels, I was using some word cards I had bought at the Bounty Bookstore. They were supposed to be for little children who were learning to read, one word at a time, as Tris was. Just at the edge of the frame of the photograph, among the debris, there was a supposedly haphazard scattering of the cards that I had gently arranged to read "I WANT TO HAVE YOU HERE WITH ME". But when the prints came back from One Hour Photo (which took three days), I saw that in my carefully casual arrangement of the cards I had accidentally let the word "NOT" peek through, so the photograph quite clearly read, "I WANT TO HAVE YOU *NOT* HERE WITH ME".

I showed it to Fiona. "Well, that's just it, isn't it?" she said. She was pouring boiling water on an overly brazen and foolhardy cockroach, which is what she and her children did at their house to kill them.

"We *want* to have them. You *want* Jonathan and I *want* Piers"—her boyfriend in England—"but not here with us." Not here, in the place we had found on our own, that was ours alone. Fiona and I were so close now, like sisters, bonded by our shared experience. Would Jonathan or Piers ever really understand what our lives here had been like?

Later Fiona photographed me with her pinhole camera again. I was curled up on my side on her bed, naked except for a garland of shell necklaces. She had rigged the camera to the ceiling fan above the bed. I was supposed to stay still for the long exposure, but we had to do it over twice— once because a breeze came in and caught the fan blades and they swung around, and once because I heard Fiona screech, "Oskar—stay *out*!!" which caused me to move.

You don't go off to the South Pacific because of how terrific the technology is, or because you're hoping to encounter really state-of-the-art appliances. You should have a fairly high degree of comfort with rust, obsolescence and hand-cranking. Even at our house, where we had electricity most of the time, we had a refrigerator that fought a losing battle with the heat every afternoon and a dead computer. There was also a telephone and a transistor radio. We had a washing machine that Emily admonished me never to put the children's muddy sneakers into, and we dried our clothes (when it wasn't raining) on a line stretched out on the west side of the house, just out of the shade of the guava trees. There was an oven in Emily's kitchen and a hot plate in ours; we both had electric kettles and toasters. There was a ceiling fan in our bedroom, but not in any others.

Eventually we had to get a new washing machine. Emily was not pleased about this: Frank had bought her the existing washing machine, and when he had bought it twenty-eight years before it had been the best one to be had on the island. In fact, it was the only one to be had on the island. But for years now it had had to be filled by running a rubber hose into it from the laundry sink, and finally it had stopped agitating the clothes altogether. We had to stir them around in the feebly soapy water with the top half of an old rowboat oar that was otherwise used to prop open the laundry window. It would have been almost as easy to take the clothes across the road to the beach and beat them on the rocks, and the view would have been better.

After a month of standing over the washing machine stirring it as though it were a witch's cauldron, I drove Emily to the CITC and we purchased a new one, the cheapest one possible so that figuring out how to operate it wouldn't be too complicated. Over the course of two days, guys from the CITC came to the house and ever so slowly installed it, using an alarming amount of electrical tape, and parts that hadn't come in the original packaging. Then Mata took the old machine off to her house where it would enjoy a new life as an ice chest.

Neither Emily nor I used the new machine for a while—we didn't have the heart.

Jonathan called more frequently as time went on, and Emily often chatted with him before handing over the phone. She took his intentions towards me seriously and formed a judgment about him based on Polynesian standards: the longer he was willing to stay on the line with her (at long-distance, international rates) talking endlessly about nothing in particular, the better a person he was. In the end, she approved. She was so pleased to have romance in the house again, even if it came from twelve time zones away.

Despite this long-distance romance, though, I needed to get out more. Life was tranquil: I woke at dawn and put the children and myself to bed not long after dark. But there were other worlds on the island, and some of them were apparently quite wild. One Monday the newspaper ran a story, "Boxers Take First Step to Oceania", about the qualifying rounds for selection of boxers to compete in the biannual Oceania Championships in Tahiti. The event had taken place in a bar called Banana Court. From the report, it had been a madhouse. The evening had started off with an exhibition bout by "former boxers Pastor Nio Mare and Piri Puruto", the latter of whom I happened to know was at least seventy years old. There had been an injury in the first real match, and the second match had had to be stopped when one of the fighters "outclassed" the other. There had also been damage in a "one-sided affair in the Super Heavy Weight section— 91 kg and over".

Things had gone downhill—or uphill, depending on your point of view—from there. Members of the audience had begun to spontaneously "participate", which I guess evened things out some, and a former Cook Islands champion, Pupuke Robati Jnr, had made an appearance against William Cuthers in a closely fought bout. There had, however, been some confusion about who had won and all hell had broken loose. I tried to imagine it—a dark night under the Banana Court's yellow light bulbs and the ceiling fans that didn't manage to break the heat of the bodies packed inside.

The article included a photo of Tu Potoru, one of the Super Heavy Weight fighters, looking like a giant and landing a punch on his hapless opponent, but the image was pale and lifeless compared to the sweaty chaos conjured up in my mind.

About this time, I decided that the boys and I should start doing some of the tourist activities on the island. We had never really taken advantage of all that was offered. I had been too preoccupied with our housing problems when we first arrived and too happy staying home after that.

We began to work our way through the activities suggested in our guidebook, sometimes taking Emily, or Mata and Kali, with us. We went to "Island Night" buffets at the big hotels. (Fortunately, they excluded sea cucumbers.) We attended dancing shows, waving to our friends as they stepped out on stage in their grass skirts, and laughing uproariously when tourists were coaxed on to the stage with them. No sane person should ever put him- or herself in a position where they can be compared, in terms of grace and sensuality, with an eighteen-year-old Polynesian dancer.

We went horse riding. We took the "Lagoon Cruise", which was filled with wan honeymoon couples. We went to the Cultural Village and watched a man put on a display of husking a drinking coconut just the way Mata always did.

The activities made me feel uneasy: they seemed extra bright, extra colorful. They weren't false exactly, more like a shiny coat the island wore to protect its real warm pliant body from the onslaught of tourists.

Saturday, March 15

Mata has had a fight with Rupert and left him. In my opinion, this is not a bad thing. Mata has a good heart. Perhaps Rupert has good qualities too, but they are hidden. Well hidden. Very well hidden. "I make him happy," Mata says to me. I try not to picture just exactly what making Rupert happy might involve.

This time he threatened her with a knife. Then he went to her little house in Avatiu and hammered on the door, shouting drunken threats through the window and waving the knife at the woman living there. She wouldn't let him in and told him Mata was not there.

Now he thinks that she is here with us, which she is. He doesn't dare come here, but he calls on the phone two or three times a day, asking Emily if Mata is here. Emily tells him no, but he knows that she is. She is sleeping on the little low bed in Emily's workroom.

"You will stay with us here," Emily said to Mata in the early morning light in the kitchen. "He's an old fool," Mata said to me later, with a studied air of tough-guy nonchalance—helped considerably by the fact she was wielding a machete, splitting the top off a coconut with a huge whacking chop and handing it to me to drink.

She isn't going to work at night at the Paradise Inn any more; Rupert has gone there twice, drunk, looking for her. Instead, she is working in our garden, mowing the lawn and raking the rubbish. Emily had earlier hired three fishermen to trim the hedges and prune the trees. They were off a Korean fishing boat that had been caught fishing illegally and impounded back to Rarotonga until the crew had spent enough money in the bars to make up for the fish. The men pulled out heaps of tangled vines, but stopped when they found wasp nests (Mata calls them "whops nests") and one got stung. Emily marched out and sprayed the nests with insect repellent while the Korean fisherman sat on the ground and looked on in

horror. She then beat down the nests and burned
them. The wasps buzzed around bewildered for a while,
looking for their nests, but eventually flew away.
Meanwhile, they had stung Emily, too. She took some
sap from the au tree at the foot of the drive and put it
on the stings. She says it also works for jellyfish. It
seems to me a rather thin fallback to justify such
daring.

The Koreans left without getting paid. We owe
them $63. Emily put the money in an envelope, gave it
to Mata and sent her down to the harbour to try to
find them. Mata didn't know whom to look for
because the men had been here for only one and a half
days, and that was before the fight with Rupert, and
we didn't know their names. When Mata couldn't find
them, Emily gave the money to Peter, her angel from
the Lord, who had stopped by to see if she was needing
any help with anything. Peter had never seen the
Koreans and also didn't know their names, but
somehow it seemed a step in the right direction.

Peter has been around a lot lately; he's building
a shed over a toilet in the yard east of the house.
Emily is thinking of eventually making this shed into
a self-contained apartment. This is rather visionary
on her part. The toilet isn't connected to anything: it
just sits in a corner of the yard gathering fallen
avocado leaves in its bowl. Water pools after a rain

and the leaves slowly decompose into slime and algae.
I pour in cooking oil on the sly every now and then
because someone told me that oil floating on the
surface of water keeps mosquitoes from breeding.

Peter is having troubles at home. His wife is
drinking a lot. He is thinking of becoming a Mormon.
"Do you drink?" he asked me yesterday while we were
sitting together on the steps, looking out at the palm
trees and the bright blue sky and the toilet. "No," I
lied, wondering how much he might have heard from
Elder Smith and Elder Winston. "Just a glass of wine
every now and then." We were waiting for lunch.
With Peter and Mata around, Emily has been cooking
lunch for us all—ika mata, baked octopus, taro,
rukau, corned beef and stewed sea cucumber guts. The
only problem—well, other than the stewed guts—is
that she cooks it at six a.m. and then it sits around on
the porch for five or six hours while the flies mate on
it and the temperature creeps up and the food
congeals and starts to smell.

Emily loads the table, grumbling and happy to
be cooking for us all. Peter and I flit around behind
her trying to figure out what is least likely to poison
us. "I'm not eating that," Mata laughs. She goes to
Raro Fried Chicken and comes back with something
that doesn't look as much like fried rats as the things
they usually sell me. Aiden and Tris eat with Mata.

Emily eats the octopus. Last night she was sick and today she went to the doctor for antibiotics. She's certain she has caught something.

I have been making Mata coffee in the mornings. "Would you like some coffee?" I ask her on the veranda. "Yes, please," she says in the gravelly, slurred voice that so perplexed me when I first heard it.

There is a coffee plantation on Atiu, an island about 180 kilometres to the north-east, but it is almost impossible to get real coffee at the CITC because everyone drinks Nescafé. There are a few bags of ground coffee on a dusty shelf. They are flavoured. I always buy the toffee-flavoured kind. I make Mata's toffee coffee with lots of milk and lots of sugar.

"You make the best coffee of anyone," Mata says. This is funny because Kay came last week to sit in my kitchen and have coffee with me. She took a sip and then said, very politely, "I think your milk's gone off."

"Oh," I said, "no—it's just the toffee coffee." I smiled reassuringly and took a big scalding gulp from my own cup to show her it was safe, choking at the end and spilling coffee on my green University of the South Pacific T-shirt.

"Oh," she said. "I thought the milk had gone off."

"No," I said, still choking a little, "not yet."

We have the $63 in an envelope pinned to the
calendar on the kitchen wall in case the Korean
fishermen ever come back to get it.

Wednesday, March 19
   Mata has gone back to Rupert.
   The self-contained apartment fell down yesterday
because of the high wind and the fact that it wasn't
attached to the ground in any way. Peter has decided
not to become a Mormon after all and is getting along
better with his wife.

Even though we were both of us now committed to long-
distance overseas romances, Fiona and I spent more and
more time with Ted and Nate. It was a dangerous game in
many ways. I never saw Nate's wife around but she was
there. Nate and I were less bashful with each other now,
but much more furtive.

I would catch a look in Fiona's eye sometimes, a silent
recognition that we had formed a secret sisterhood. We
didn't talk about it—at least not directly—even with each
other, but we were both torn between the warm and
loving men who were waiting for us on the other side of
the world and the dangerous men who were waiting for us
on the other side of town.

Ted was putting together a show of old photographs
from the library's archives, and asked Fiona and me to

help him choose them. We spent about three hours late one day looking through books of antique pictures. The library was closed, so we had the whole place to ourselves. The kids hung around being nice kids—Aiden and Oskar played chess and Alma read to Tris. After a while, Nate came by and he and Ted took us all to dinner at Trader Jack's. I got the feeling the two men spent a lot of time there. The crowd at the bar welcomed them warmly, and we got a large table looking out over the harbour. Polynesians are among the largest people on Earth. Sitting next to these men, Fiona and I seemed like children and the actual children seemed like butterflies. Ted talked to Alma about her new boyfriend, listening very intently. Nate and Fiona and I talked about art and passion. It seemed very profound, but that may have been the wine.

Every morning, I would write part of a letter to Jonathan. As the boys played on the veranda or climbed guava trees outside the window, I would sit at the kitchen table with a pen and a pad of airmail stationery and grope for the right words. I hadn't seen Jonathan for fifteen years, apart from one day the year before when he had briefly visited me in Colorado. When he had got off the plane, he had looked just the same as he used to. And when I kissed him hello, he tasted just like he had fourteen years before—like fresh-baked cookies and summer rain. It had all come flooding back to me.

Tuesday, March 25

Emily has just come in to tell me that she is going down the driveway to give a piece of her mind to the nice young couple who have rented the caretaker's house. They haven't done anything out of line—they are very quiet, prompt with the rent, and have done quite a bit of much-needed maintenance on the place. But Emily has gone to tell them that if they won't pay the rent, there are plenty of people who will. Not that they are late with the rent, or have ever been late with the rent, but some former tenants used to be late with the rent and she says she doesn't want these people to get to be like those people. So she has gone to lay down the law. Sometimes Emily has a strong streak of the querulous in her.

I just went into the kitchen to make myself a cup of tea and two moko were having sex on the windowsill. They kept at it and watched me make my tea. It cheered me up. I've learned a lot about our creature friends while living here.

It was becoming quite convivial at the house. Now that Lena had moved in and visitors came by more often, we were not nearly as secluded as we had been.

March 27 was Emily's eighty-third birthday. We took her out to eat at Paulina's Polynesian Restaurant, along with Mata and Lena. Lena made us all 'ei katu to wear and the boys and I wore our silk-screened clothes. We gave Emily a hammock on a stand to put out in the yard. She had been talking a lot lately about how she would like to lie in the cool shade of the tipani trees. We set up the hammock for her in the front garden, in the shade. She got into it okay but then she couldn't get out, so we tried to rig up something with a pareu to help her get herself out when I wasn't there. Aiden and Tris then took over the hammock and spent the rest of the afternoon swinging in it. Emily seemed relieved.

ALIENS

Born and bred Americans often have a pretty narrow view of the world. There was a story with which my brother Joe and I loved to regale people after our visit to Indonesia. We had left Jakarta by train, travelling further into the interior of the island of Java. Because of the cholera epidemic and the rush of people trying to get out of the city, the train station was chaotic and Joe, nothing if not gallant, stood against a wall with the luggage while I made my way through the jostling throng to the ticket counter. He was leaning against the wall watching my progress when a gregariously drunk man approached and asked where he was from.

The man then said, "You know it is our Independence Day today?"

"Yes," Joe said.

"We are independent forty years today," the man said.

"Yes, I know," Joe said.

"Is America independent?" the man asked, squinting curiously up at Joe.

"Yes, it is."

"How long?" he asked challengingly.

"Two hundred years," Joe said.

The man whistled appreciatively. "Is long time," he said. He nodded, graciously ceding precedence, and stumbled off.

Back home, Joe and I gleefully told this story over and over again, thinking it was funny that someone would not know the US had been independent for a very long time. We thought this because we were stupid. We had all the infantile arrogance of children raised in a superpower who assume their country is so important that everyone in the world knows about it.

Of course this is not true. The US didn't matter in the Cooks, where if people looked to any outside countries they looked to New Zealand and sometimes Australia. Occasionally they vilified France, justifiably, for performing nuclear tests upwind of Pukapuka, the group's northern atoll. US government policies didn't affect the Cooks in any discernible way and US news didn't interest its inhabitants. It was rather a relief not to be automatically despised as an ugly American—no one thought about Americans enough to even stereotype them. If the newspaper ever had a story with an American dateline, it was invariably in the page two column devoted to the weird and the humorous.

Over time I lost all contact with the political and economic goings-on in my native country; the only news I got was the weather report from Arkansas, which my father included in his weekly email. In late March, however, the US intruded itself, via the daily newspaper, into my consciousness. *Cook Islands News* was generally a source of baffled mirth—a surreal collection of the slapstick, the bewildering, the befuddled and the macabre. On March 29, for example, the headline on its front page read: "Marlin caught off Ngatangiia". This was accompanied by a photograph of an 82.8-kilogram marlin sticking out the back end of Junior Ioaba's pickup truck. It had been landed after a three-hour battle.

"Of interest," the story reported, "is that the marlin had a long-line hook embedded in the left side of its mouth." I guess it had tangled with humans before and eventually, as for all of us, that can only lead to trouble. It certainly looked dead there in the back of the truck, and surprised—but, really, fish almost always look that way.

But then, on page two, was another headline: "Baghdad bombed again". This truly was news to me, as I didn't know it had been bombed the first time. Apparently my homeland had gone to war. George W. Bush was quoted saying, "Against this enemy we will accept no outcome except complete victory."

Did that sound as false and callow in the US as it did in Rarotonga?

"In Baghdad," the report went on, "a doctor at Al Noor Hospital said he counted fifty-five people killed and more than forty-seven wounded from an air raid at the busy market in Baghdad's Shula neighborhood, which could undermine American efforts to win Iraqi hearts and minds." Well, yes. Using cruise missiles to kill women while they are out buying eggplants—that *does* get people's backs up.

I showed the newspaper to Emily, who was as surprised as I was—about the war, anyway; she said she had seen bigger marlin. She looked at Aiden and Tris with quiet concern and emphasised that I was not to allow them to be dragged off to war. She told me repeatedly, speaking very gravely so I would be sure to understand, to bring them back to Rarotonga where we would all live peacefully together out of harm's way.

"No one bothers us here," she said.

I didn't know then that we were hearing about the start of the war without end. As I write, it is still going on. I thought, looking into the faces of my children that I had nothing to worry about: they would never be dragged off to fight in an insanely stupid war. Perhaps I was foolish to believe we had nothing to fear from any damage the Bush

White House could inflict on the world. I have learned. My children still have the same long-lashed green eyes, but sometimes now when I look into them a chill grips my heart and I have to clutch them tightly to me.

Could we have lived without this fear if we had stayed on the island—or, at least, not come back to the US? Or was it an illusion to think we could escape all the turmoil and dread of the outside world by hiding in our tropical Shangri-La? If we hadn't gone to the world, would the world have come to us?

At the time the Iraq war seemed ludicrous, a mistake that would be cleared up quickly because it was so absurd that it had been started at all. We heard nothing about the Orwellian nightmare into which America was sinking, nothing about the spying and the torture and the secret prisons and the whipping up of hysterical fear. Its leaders seemed as aberrant as the leaders of Nauru who had allowed their country to become lost. It was difficult to believe that such a high level of insanity would be allowed to continue for long. I wish I had the luxury of believing that now.

I wonder what will happen to us all? What level of destruction is waiting for my children in their future? And will Rarotonga survive it—peacefully out of harm's way, as Emily promised us—or will it be just another casualty? It was almost lost once before, when the missionaries came. The diseases they brought killed off ninety percent of the population, and with them lots of knowledge about the original pantheon of gods and forms of dance and music. It is an exceedingly fragile sanctuary.

There were three things Aiden and Tris became very aware of while we were on the island that they had been barely, if at all, aware of before: death, drunkenness and Jesus. And, of course, it made perfect sense that those three things should end up grouped together. They often are. After months helping Mata raise her pigs and seeing wild dogs lurking around the nests of the baby chicks, the boys were under no illusions about what meat was. After our car wreck they had first-hand acquaintance with drunks. And after living with Mormon missionaries, they certainly knew what Christians were.

I was perplexed by the motivations of the original missionaries to the South Seas, unable to understand their zeal for changing this culture. John Williams, the leader of the London Missionary Society in the South Pacific, went from island to island converting people at a frantic pace until he was finally eaten by the people of Erromango in Vanuatu. Meanwhile, though, life had changed for the islanders. Emily dug out one of her mother's corsets from a trunk in the workroom and showed it to me. It was a remnant of missionary rule, a tangled contraption of metal stays, rusty hooks and rotting canvas. Christ, I thought, as a trickle of sweat slowly made its way down my spine, I can't even stand to put on *socks*. Who, in their right mind, would force such torturous garments on to the daughters of Eve?

I imagined John Williams as a product of industrial capitalism in nineteenth-century Europe, helping export all the inadequacies of that system to a place to which they had not been invited. It occurred to me that this was just like Bush's war on Islam. The world the boys and I had left behind, where freezing people huddled over subway vents, bullied outcasts shot their classmates in hallways, spoiled heiresses plowed SUVs into crowds outside night-clubs, many children went hungry, and a moronic president cheated his way into office without regard for the democracy he supposedly valued highly for other countries —why would anyone think it worthwhile to export that to anywhere else?

I wrote Jonathan a long letter going deeply into these thoughts, and the connections I saw between the London Missionary Society and the American war against Iraq. I mentioned the letter to Fiona. She looked horrified. "You didn't *mail* it, did you?" she said.

The news from the US continued to be an almost unfathomable combination of the grim and the surreal. The next day a story on page two of the newspaper reported that things didn't seem to be going quite the way Bush had thought they would. The army had become bogged down outside Basra, a city in the south. A com-mander was quoted as saying, "The planning assumption had always been that the advancing forces would simply sweep past Basra and it would implode by itself." I especially liked the combination of the words "assumption", "simply" and "by itself". It did not seem the hallmark of really top-notch military strategising.

Also on page two was a story from London headed "Harris Hawk Harry Hoists Hairpiece". The key sentence was: "The problems began when Harry, a Harris hawk, flew off with a spectator's toupée and tried to eat it, thinking it was live prey." I loved this. It really said something about the quality of fake hair in Britain. Something like this could happen on Rarotonga of course, but at least there when someone wore something on his head that looked like live prey, it was live prey. From my perspective on the veranda, page two, taken all together, made it seem as though the outside world was being directed by Fellini.

On a happier note, a nine-petal tipani had been found in Oliver and Joyce Peyroux's garden in Avaavaroa. One photo had a close-up of the flower, and another showed a young woman wearing it behind her ear. There was also a brief discussion of other remarkable flowers. A nine-petalled tiare had, for example, been found at the High Commissioner's residence the year before. So while World War III was being whipped up on the other side of the planet, in our small tropical sanctuary people were out in their gardens looking carefully at the flowers and calling the newspaper to report anything unusual. I thought

Aiden, Tris and I were very lucky. It was as though we were living on a distant mountain, but with a clear view of Vesuvius erupting. I hoped the smoke wouldn't get us.

Wednesday, April 2

   Aiden is working on a drawing of Jesus that he intends to attach to a crucifix he has made out of straws. This is because I told him I am going to photograph a sea cucumber and he is very, very upset about that; he is planning to show the crucifix with Jesus on it to the sea cucumber while it is having its picture taken "to help it not to die" while it is out of the water. He is singing "Hark! The Herald Angels Sing" while he draws, and Tris has just asked, "Can I draw Jesus, too?" I don't encourage too much Christianity in the children, scarred as I am by the venal actions of American fundamentalists, but here it is just a part of our lives.

   Tris is now posing for Aiden with his arms outspread. I am going to take a picture of this and forget about the sea cucumber.

I started to see more and more of Nate at the same time that my head was filled almost exclusively with longing for Jonathan. Nate was increasingly charming and I was increasingly charmed, but I wasn't so silly as to think that I was anything other than a pleasant diversion for him, or that stepping into the roiling sea of sex and jealousy on the island would do anything other than drown me. An artist I interviewed told me the younger women on the island got drunk and physically fought each other over men. "Men!" she scoffed disdainfully. I didn't think I was up to it.

Nate was applying for an artist's fellowship and he asked me if I would write a letter of recommendation for him. I stopped by his house with it one morning. His wife was standing in the kitchen washing their daughter's hair. She seemed angry—angry at me for being there, angry at Nate for being there, angry at her daughter's hair for being there. She was scrubbing at it fiercely, with a look on her face like a gorgeous, very mad bird of prey.

I thought it would be best to make myself agreeable. "Gosh," I said, all kid-sweet and fake-friendly, "that's nice-smelling shampoo." The little girl shot me a withering look. "It's for lice," she snapped.

Saturday, April 5

Tris is playing a game and singing to himself: "Mosquito man, mosquito man / He can do whatever a mosquito can!"

The boys and I spent a while this morning straightening up our room, which has become a repository of seashells, library books, rocks, feathers, things covered in sand, and delicate constructions involving clothespins and string. A couple of hours later when I went in, there was a teetering castle constructed of books and driftwood in the middle of the floor. "What's all this?" I said. Aiden was reclining on my bed reading the newspaper. He looked at me over the top of the pages and cocked one eyebrow. "Trissy abhors a vacuum," he said.

Yesterday, the boys were talking together in the back seat of the car. Aiden said, "I'm thinking of a number between one and fifteen. You have five questions to guess it." Tris thought about it for a minute or two and then said, "Well, my first question is: what is the number?"

Jonathan and I began to plan out some way of actually seeing each other. Some plans travelled by letter, some by email, and some through our increasingly frequent phone calls. The letter plans took weeks to arrive, and were superseded before they were even read by the email plans I received every Monday, which themselves were superseded by the even more immediate phone call plans. At any one moment, plans, schemes and ideas were all mixed together in a frothy ferment of love and desire and wild impracticality, fuelled by a giddy feeling that we had always been meant to be together and that the only things standing between us and perfect happiness were time and space. I got letters from Jonathan suggesting schemes in which I would fly to Paris and he would take the train and meet me there. We would hole up in a hotel and spend long hours making love, emerging only every now and then to eat in out-of-the-way cafés and stare deeply into each other's eyes. (These were the first plans I made that acknowledged that I would someday be leaving the island.)

The impracticality of these types of ideas—where, for example, would Aiden and Tris be?—seemed trivial in the face of our desire to be together. Interminable time, immense space and no money are picky details that all new lovers think can be easily overcome with a stroke of genius. One inventive idea, one solution dreamt up in a flash of insight, and all obstacles are swept away, if you only believe. And after all South Sea islands were only dreams too. There was no telling what passion could accomplish.

One Saturday we went with Fiona, Oskar and Alma to the market. We were taking bags of guavas to Emily's cousin who had a fruit and vegetable stall. Maybe the tourists would buy them. The same cousin had recently come by and hauled off a bunch of our avocados for sale in the cold room of the CITC. At the market, Fiona wanted to buy a stem of bananas. Bananas came off the tree this way— dozens and dozens attached to a long stem. The banana stem was really lovely and Fiona wanted to photograph it, but afterwards she and the children would have had to eat all the quickly rotting bananas. We stopped by their house a few days later to see how it was going. Oskar and Alma were looking doleful.

Friday, April 11

It's Friday afternoon and I've just finished drinking a coconut. Most of the morning, the boys and I ran errands—or at least tried to. We had about a twenty percent success rate, which is pretty good for us. The art gallery that is open M-F 10-6 was closed yesterday afternoon at three and closed today at 11:30. The Government Statistics office, where I needed some final information, was open, in that the door was standing open, but it was devoid of human beings. We waited futilely for about a half an hour, then left and went to the grocery store. The CITC was open and had people in it but was running short on groceries: we needed milk and garlic but they didn't have either. The bookstore didn't have any newspapers and the bank didn't have any two-dollar coins. However, the bakery had two loaves of bread left and the lagoon is ten shades of particularly lovely turquoise today, so it all evens out.

Very quickly now, the time approached for Fiona to leave the island and go back to England. I had known her for only a few months, but it seemed as though we had been part of each other forever. Maybe we were truly kindred spirits. Maybe the island made everyone feel that way. Maybe each of us had spent so much time being strong and brave for the sake of our children that when we found each other we just collapsed together: at the very least we would not be alone any more. Finding a comrade in arms has a heady effect.

Fiona made Emily very happy by paying her two hundred dollars for the blanket that Emily used to cover her work table when she was silk-screening clothes. It was an old wool blanket that had been there for years protecting the table. The paint from the silk screens always bled through a little and left a shadow image on the surface below, so the blanket was now a dense palimpsest of tiare māori and hibiscus and tikis and the image of a little thatched hut village nestled under the palms. I saw the blanket every day, and sometimes when it was raining I spread the clothes out on it to dry, but I didn't see how beautiful it was until Fiona pointed it out. That was Fiona's true gift—seeing beauty in things that other people blindly passed by.

At first Emily was completely overwhelmed and embarrassed when Fiona wanted to buy the blanket. She blushed and hid her face in her hands and went scampering off to the kitchen. I followed her and, after much whispered plotting, emerged as the intermediary. I whisked the unseemly loot back to the kitchen where Emily gleefully pocketed it while Fiona was stowing the blanket in her car.

Then we all appeared back together and Emily pressed a banana cake and a big bag of guavas on Fiona in order to erase the knowledge that she had sold something she considered valueless for an ungodly sum of money. But both Fiona and I knew that Fiona had got a great deal. Emily was all fired up now to make replica blankets and sell them to the tourists, but there would never be another one like Fiona's. It was unique in the world.

Fiona was more than happy to part with her two hundred dollars. She had been on a buying jag as her departure date loomed. She had paid twice that for a red glass statue of Tangaroa, the god of the sea, which the Beachcomber Gallery hadn't been planning to sell until she talked them into it with the lure of a ridiculous amount of cash. It was tempting to keep buying beautiful things in the hope of somehow getting the talisman, the magic pebble that would allow you to hold Rarotonga in your hand. Then you would never have to really leave.

After Emily went off to town to put her windfall in the bank, Fiona lingered on the veranda for a long time, debating with me back and forth if it could somehow be possible for us to stay. "No, it's im-*poss*-ible," she said over and over again, not very convincingly.

"You could marry Ted," I proposed. "I could marry Nate and you could marry Ted. You would be the queen. I would come to visit you at the palace and we would have tea."

Fiona giggled. "Oh, they would never let a white

woman be queen," she said. Of course she was right. It was impossible. "And besides," she said, more solemnly, "there's no school for the children—the clever children all have to be sent away…"

But we stayed thinking about it a long time. From the outside it must have seemed crazy to leave the sun, sea and languid life in paradise and go back to crowded, noisy, dirty, grim civilisation. But it wasn't that simple. We didn't need words to explain it to ourselves, just the image of Nate's angry wife, the stench of stale whisky on the driver who hit us, the way the ladies in the market saw us coming and hiked up the prices.

Not even that—we just knew that it would all be so different, so much harder, if we were staying. The demands of a Polynesian family are imperious, the responsibilities like a rug that wraps you up warm and cozy and then slowly suffocates you. "You are ours," the family says, and it's both a great comfort and a terrible threat.

History never went away on the island and no one ever forgot your past, although they always came to forgive you for it in time. It was a hard place to live for a woman who might want to make some mistakes. For all its risks and hazards, there's something to be said for freedom. Emily's weren't the only children who had gone away and chosen never to come back.

So when Fiona stood, hesitating, on the steps of the veranda and said, "It's im-*poss*-ible", we both knew it was true. We had come there following a wild dream of the fierce ocean wind—looking for escape, or just to go somewhere, anywhere, else. Just to go. But the open sea was always still out there, and the island was so small there was only so far you could travel in a ceaseless circle around the edge of it. This was not the island at the end of the world, finally. It was only one moment along the way. All over Polynesia, people say their ancestors came to the islands from a homeland—on Rarotonga it is called Ava'iki—and their souls will return there when they die. On Rarotonga, the souls of the dead depart from Black Rock every night and head out into the darkness to go home. No one knows any more exactly where Ava'iki is— you are told a hundred different directions if you ask—but at the ends of their lives they must make that journey. Fiona and I were really no different—in our hearts we were searching for a lost paradise.

Fiona sighed and then blushed. "It's so much easier falling in love with women," she said, "don't you think?" I knew what she meant. She and I could love each other, as one inevitably loves one's travelling companions. You meet on the road, travel together for a while, and then part eventually. But you never forget.

I could make a long list of people I fell in love with while I lived on the island: Jonathan and Nate, Fiona and Oskar and Alma and Ted, Emily and Mata and Malcolm and Nga, Lee and Ian and Tim Buchanan, and other people that I haven't told you about. The more I think, the longer the list grows.

In the middle of April, Fiona left. She was headed for the US and then home to England. She wasn't quite ready to leave. It was easy to see how someone could tie up at the harbour, come ashore to get fresh water and still be there twenty years later. Just about every long-term expatriate I spoke to had originally planned to stay only a week or ten days. They were all just not quite ready to leave yet. Like Fletcher Christian, you stop in for a few breadfruit saplings, and the next thing you know you've commandeered the ship and thrown the captain overboard—anything to stay just a little longer.

Ted came to the house late in the morning the day after Fiona left. She had told him he should spend more time with me—that he needed someone from the outside to talk to. We discussed Jane Austen, whom he said was his favorite author. It was funny to think of this descendant of Polynesian chiefs sitting in his jungle house in the middle of sacred grounds reading *Sense and Sensibility* while moko looked over his shoulder.

Then he asked me if I were missing Fiona and I burst into tears. "Terribly," I snuffled, suddenly feeling that I was. Ted, being stoic, did not cry but he did get a bit misty around the edges.

Both Emily and Lena arrived home. They seemed a bit shocked to find me weeping on the porch in an audience with the possible successor to the ariki. Ted said he wanted to come over the next night with a bottle of wine. He said, "We will talk about many things." All I could think of was: "'The time has come,' the walrus said / 'to talk of many things / Of shoes and ships and sealing wax / Of cabbages and kings'." I didn't pass this thought along to Ted, however. After he left Emily said, "He seems like such a nice boy. His mother used to talk about him all the time—she loved him so."

Thursday, April 17

It has been a tropically hot day. Now it's evening I'm sitting in the slowly darkening kitchen watching a moko eat a housefly. The boys are blowing bubbles out in the garden. Tris especially is beside himself with joy. He looks like a bright sprite dancing around in the twilight, a creature of pure happiness. Watching them play, I feel as though I have a handful of Eden.

With Fiona gone, I found myself spending more time with Kara and Lee. Lee occasionally showed up somewhere in a suit and tie, having made some compelling argument about injustice or otherwise attended to the interests of the downtrodden in the full regalia befitting his station, but mostly he attended to the downtrodden's interests just fine in shorts and flip-flops. Kara, on the other hand, wore high heels to the beach and never got her face wet. She knew, of course, about the unfulfilled crushes that Fiona and I harboured towards Ted and Nate—there was no secret on the tiny island that was safe from a determined woman—and mocked us, all in good fun she claimed, for our pathetic and hopeless desires. But I noticed that she looked at Ted a lot when we were all together and laughed very hard at his jokes.

Aiden, Tris and I went on a hike with Kara, Lee and Ella into the interior and up the side of a mountain called Raemaru. Living as we did on the edge of the coast, it was amazing to be really in the jungle. First of all, it was pretty dark: the vegetation was so thick it seemed almost carnivorous; I could hear ferns licking their lips as we passed by. I expected the plant from *Little Shop of Horrors* to jump out of the foliage and burst into a rousing rendition of "Feed Me, Seymour".

The climb was surprisingly tough. In some places the undergrowth, with its massive leaves, was over Tris's head. At one point Aiden stepped off the edge of a drop-off hidden by plants and was suddenly hanging by his hands over a deep, black crevice. Fortunately he didn't weigh much, so the ferns he grabbed supported his weight. After a moment—maybe it was a millisecond but it seemed like a year—of total paralysis on the part of all the adults, Lee and I hauled him out and the plants sprang back into place. The crevice was hidden again, waiting patiently for the next potential meal.

After a couple of minutes, Aiden was no longer scared. In fact he had started to think it was fun. Tris and Ella wanted to try. "*I* want to plunge to my death! *I* want to plunge to my death. Please! Oh, please, please, *please*!" We had snacks instead. I had brought guavas from the tree outside our kitchen window. It was producing fruit by the truckload: even Mata's pigs were starting to get sick of them. "Oh, guavas," Lee said. "I love guavas." I told him I would bring him some, as though I were doing him a big favour. I wondered how many I could fit in the car.

One of the nice things about living on Rarotonga was that we almost always had whatever place we were at to ourselves. The beach was always empty, for example. In the jungle we didn't see or hear anyone else. We didn't even see signs of anyone else. (The plants ate the bones and clothing too I guess.) There was an overwhelming, velvety silence. We were out for only two hours, but we returned completely wet from humidity and sweat, and covered in mud.

Sunday, April 6

A storm is blowing in. It's warm, but very windy. Tris is building with Lego. He just sat back for a minute, looked appraisingly at his construction, said "Magnificent!" and went back to work. He told me during dinner that he had tasted the cat-food for Emily's cat and it was "dee-licious!"

I like getting mail—not bills and advertising circulars but real mail such as announcements of new babies and postcards from people who have been thinking about me. It is a testament to the knee-weakening nature of love letters that the ones from Jonathan had the power to vanquish even the blue eyes of Nate Flynn.

He began to send packages. He even managed to get a box of Swiss chocolates to us without their turning into a puddle. The boys and I gobbled them down with Emily, Lena and Mata in about five minutes and then felt light-headed.

And he sent books for Aiden and Tris. My original idea had been that I would home-school the boys because the school curricula on the island concentrated heavily on teaching cleanliness and godliness (in my opinion, two of life's lesser accomplishments) to the detriment of teaching, say, mathematics. In general, however, I have to say that home-schooling was pretty much a failure.

When I was planning our trip, I thought we would have internet access and I would be able to get what I needed online. So many things turned out to be different from how I imagined they would be. Tris's school became the garden and the seashore. Aiden taught himself Pitman shorthand from an old book of Emily's. But mostly they just ran wild and climbed trees and played. Jonathan sent us a book of science experiments that we tried to perform, although we often couldn't get the equipment we needed (plastic strawberry baskets, Epsom salts...). Sometimes I got the boys to write notes about our adventures. They also made up poems. Aiden wrote a long poem about worms, a very short poem about roosters —"I wonder why the rooster crows? / I guess that that is all he knows" —and a funny poem about imagining life under the sea.

My father sent a book of children's poetry with a Robert Louis Stevenson poem:

I should like to rise and go
Where the golden apples grow
Where below another sky
Parrot islands anchored lie.

It was the poem I had painted on to the wall of our hallway in Colorado to sustain us when we were making plans to go to our own parrot island.

The night he brought over a bottle of wine, Ted asked if I would help him cut the mats for the pictures we had chosen for the exhibition, so a few nights later the boys and I met him at the library after it closed. It was very stormy out, with lightning and thunder. Maybe it was all the wetness or electricity in the air that called forth the ancestors. Whatever the reason, they were in abundant evidence, crawling out of the ancient vaka that sat in the middle of the museum floor. They looked remarkably like big, hairy spiders. Ted said his grandmother had always told him that the spiders were the spirits of the ancestors. "Don't step on them," he warned. This seemed unlikely to occur, what with me staying as far away from them as possible without actually standing outside in the rain.

Emily had found an eight-inch-long stinging centipede in her bed late one night. "What did you do?" I gasped, goggle-eyed. "I chopped it to bits with a knife from the kitchen," she said.

Ancestors be damned.

Once you were part of the society on the island, you were part of it forever. There are no outcasts among castaways: no one is going anywhere, so people have to get along. This led to a high degree of acceptance of foibles that, in other contexts, might lead to such things as burning at the stake.

This was not uncomplaining acceptance, the indulgence of a good long complaint being one of the chief entertainments available to residents. But there was little interest in really active malice, mostly because it was just too damn hot to muster the kind of purposeful action that true vindictiveness requires. And unless you were willing to engage in cannibalism, the victim of your malice would be there just the same the next day anyway, a situation which tends to take some of the edge off victory. So, despite the fact that the memberships of all the various churches added up to 115 percent of the population, society on the island was little bothered with sustained inquiries into the morals and character of its inhabitants. And as a resident you could easily find yourself being friends, even intimate long-term friends, with people whom you really, in your heart, despised.

Fiona, Kara, Lee and I once took all our children swimming in the pool at the Rarotongan Beach Resort and Spa. Lee was a friend of the owner, who had told us to come by whenever we wanted, but we went only that one time. It was not as beautiful as the beach, of course, but it had the overwhelming advantage of waiters bringing killer rum drinks to the tables at poolside. Fiona and Kara and I sat for a while under the shade of an umbrella, living the tourist life, while Lee played with the kids in the water.

After three Mango Mai Tais, Kara told us she was dissatisfied with Lee and was contemplating having an affair. She heaved an "I'm-such-a-martyr" sigh and said that if only Lee would start sleeping with someone else she would feel freer. Fiona and I both immediately volunteered for the assignment with such obvious fervour that Kara was shocked into reconsidering her position. A few days after Fiona left, Lee stopped by our house with the news that Kara was pregnant. He was thrilled.

Every now and then the boys and I went for a horseback ride at the stables on the other side of the island. After we got home one day, Aiden was prattling breathlessly to Mata about it when she said, winking at me, "Well, tell your mum that you need a horse of your own."

"Yes, my darling," I said to him, winking back at Mata. "When we come back here to live forever, your Auntie Mata will buy you a horse." Mata laughed and Aiden went off happily to contemplate the glorious future in store for him.

For Aiden and Tris, the island was now home. They had always lived there, riding horses on the beach, having the run of Emily's house and garden, watching other people come and go while we stayed on. Sometimes I would tell Kali about snow, which she had never seen, and the boys would try to look knowledgeable and assure her authoritatively of the truth of my impossible-seeming tales. However, I noticed that they paid attention too, listening to the stories of snow and ice with the same wide eyes as to the other fairy tales and legends I told them.

Now, though, I began secretly to betray them. I had known all along that we would have to leave the island some day. Our plane tickets were open-ended, but our visas and permits were for only a year. But more than that, I found that I wanted to see Jonathan. I wanted to be with him, not just in letters but in reality. Sometimes I snuck away to the Telecom office to call him in the middle of his night. We had finally decided that I would bring Aiden and Tris with me to Zürich as soon as we got back to the US. I had planned to stay on Rarotonga until July, but now I kept pushing our departure date earlier and earlier, hoping to trade one kind of paradise for another.

Tuesday, April 29

It has been raining for four days now—sometimes just steady rain, sometimes torrential, biblical downpours. The air is so wet that everything is wet. Even this piece of paper is wet. It's like writing on a sponge.

Aiden asked me when we would read more of Mary Poppins. "Later," I said. "But when?" he said. "How much longer will we have to tread in the winds of time before we reach it?"

Without Fiona, life was a bit less lively. It is a little melancholy being the ones left behind, even if you've been left behind in Eden. It was odd but true that the population of the islands had been steadily dropping since the airport opened and there was a convenient way for people to get away. On some of the outer islands, soon there would be no one left—or only the very old people who survived on the money sent back to them by their children and grandchildren from far away. On the radio there would occasionally be an announcement of the death of someone from Rarotonga who had passed away while living in New Zealand or Australia. Invariably, this would be accompanied by information on when the body would be brought back to the island for burial. "They always want to come back home," Emily would say, but increasingly even the old people were leaving the island behind. Emily had said goodbye to many of her friends, only to see them one last time when they were brought back to be lowered into the ground.

In Māori, there are two different phrases to say goodbye—one to be said by the people who are leaving and another by the people who are staying behind. It's an acknowledgement that "goodbye" is different if you are leaving than it is if you are being left. Even as we said good-bye to Fiona and stayed behind on the island, it was hard for me to imagine her being somewhere else, far away. What would this place be like, this place where the people didn't know us or care about us and our doings? I tried to picture her there, surrounded by faces different from the ones we saw every day, but I couldn't.

Thursday, May 1
Dear Fiona,

Fiona-fest continues here on the lovely island of Rarotonga and I thought I should keep you apprised of the proceedings in your honour. As per your directive, Ted showed up on my doorstep and we had a good weep together and agreed that there didn't seem to be as much sunshine around these days. He also asked me to put some of my photographs in the show he is curating at the museum. I have agreed, but only on the condition that mine hang adjacent to yours with a trail of rose petals between them. I also saw him at the Anzac Day celebrations looking shockingly dashing in a suit and tie.

Kara, in a gesture mimicking traditional Polynesian forms of ritual self-mutilation and self-debasement during times of grief, entered herself in the section of the National Dancer of the Year Competition reserved for foreigners and, to put it gently, did not win. Admittedly, she had somewhat seriously underestimated the level of competition, thinking it was a lark for tourists. There was only one actual tourist in the show, and when not on vacation she is in the corps of the Kirov Ballet. The tape of Kara dancing is now on heavy rotation on TV during breaks in the evening news. A laugh track has been added. Kara can no longer go to the grocery store in peace.

Your old car has reappeared after a suitable period of mourning, apparently spent at the panel beater. It was at the front of Rarotonga Rentals last week, sitting with all its doors open, looking very fetching and a little wanton. I have since seen a very harassed-looking couple with two small children driving around Titikaveka in it.

*The boys and I are the same as ever. The
morning after you left, Tris was playing a game in the
garden and singing to himself, "Fiona-fee, Fiona-fee,
Fiona-fee", over and over again. Aiden is reading a
book called "Practical Greek Magic". I have got caught
up taking pictures and have completely stopped doing
research. The days seem to go by quickly without ever
coming closer to the day we leave.*

*Not everything is bad since you left though. The
island is still heartbreakingly beautiful and centipede
season is over.*

C'est tout. We miss you. Take care.

Love to you all, Kathy

Instead of getting on with my research, I was mooning
around writing letters to Jonathan and gossiping on the
porch with Emily's friends. Even on Monday afternoons it
took a very great effort to work; the rest of the week it was
hopeless. Outside, the sky was blue and the air was soft.
Inside me there was turmoil. This was Jonathan's doing.
Just before a tidal wave strikes, the ocean suddenly leaves
the shore. In a similar way, all my thoughts were being
sucked away from the island and caught in an undertow
that left me in the middle of the sea.

Towards the end, I made one last gargantuan effort
and completed everything I was supposed to do. I had a

long list of data to double-check, a last few people to interview, and information from the library to copy down by hand, the photocopier being unusable during times of high humidity—that is, always. During my early isolation I had been stunningly active, but once I was drawn into the social whirl of Rarotongan life, and then long-distance love with Jonathan, my productivity declined. There is a reason that Polynesians have dozens of words for "love" and not a single one for "research".

Saturday, May 10

It's Saturday morning—sunny, breezy and peaceful. The boys are playing together—they make up endless imaginary games with elaborate rules, special codes and secret languages. Aiden creates complex back stories—myths and legends to explain the current action. Tris builds the necessary equipment, Rube Goldberg contraptions of string, clothespins, and pieces of things he has dismantled. They run around making high keening noises (Emily calls it "the children's lovely voices") and jumping off things. Occasionally, Aiden offers Tris as a human sacrifice to the gods—they have developed great proficiency at this. Foreign travel is so broadening.

I sit in the middle and look at census data for my book.

*

We went with Emily and Lena to their cousin Marlene's birthday umukai. Marlene had lots of food and wine, and there was dancing. Marlene's delicately lovely eight-year-old niece Mere danced for us but the old people were far and away the best dancers, laughing and sensuous, much more captivating than the troupes who danced for tourists at the hotels. I wanted to grow old like a Cook Islands woman, losing all my inhibitions and none of my grace.

I met a woman named Nga, who was a masseuse. We struck up an arrangement by which she would come to our house on Tuesdays and give Emily and me each a massage. Emily drank lots of wine and laughed a lot and then fell asleep in her chair. Lena and I helped her out to the car and then we drove slowly home along the road next to the brooding ocean.

Nate Flynn came to our house late one morning. I was astonished when he appeared, walking silently up our drive: I hadn't realised he knew where we lived. Emily and I were sitting on the veranda, making 'eis for a wedding at the Castaway. Nate didn't come on to the veranda; he stood in the yard, shielding his eyes against the sun with his hand, and asked if I would come to his studio to see a new series of paintings he was working on. Even though he was standing so far away, and even though Emily was there, and Aiden and Tris were buzzing around us, and Lena hadn't left yet for work, it seemed some-how that he and I were alone. He needed something he could get from me. Or maybe it was the other way around.

Emily was very still and watchful while he was asking me. After he flushed red and left, walking back down the long driveway, she was silent for a while in a thinking kind of way. Emily's mother had not wanted her to marry her first husband, Joe Browne, but after Joe had broken Emily's heart by publicly running around with many other women she had taken Emily and her daughter Elizabeth back home to her house. Then when Emily had to go to New Zealand to work for a while, she had taken care of Elizabeth.

When Emily met Frank and brought him back home with her, Frank took Elizabeth as his own daughter. He always loved her as his own, Emily said. After Emona was born, he didn't favour her: he treated the girls equally.

Frank always took care of Emily and the girls. At the end, when he knew he was dying, he didn't tell Emily how bad it was; she didn't know until the very last days that he would die.

Emily said to me that if I ever married—she said this when Jonathan had called, or when she had brought back a letter from him from the post office—I must make sure beforehand that my husband would love my children as if they were his own. She caressed my children with her eyes and with her ancient hands, touching them lightly on their hair, and said, "You must make *sure* that he loves them." And I promised.

But of course she had married Joe Browne, married him in spite of everything, so when she saw Nate Flynn standing by the steps, black-haired and blue-eyed, asking me to come to him, she understood how I felt.

I went to his studio later that day. The paintings were huge panels of ancient Māori myths. We stood close together in the afternoon sun with the old gods glowering down on us. He tried to explain to me how he was wrestling with the images, fighting with the paintings— trying to make them be the things he felt. His wife's face was in them over and over again. When I left, he stayed behind to keep working while there was still some light left. I realised he had given some of the tortured men his own face too.

I had already had my share of Joe Brownes. It was just as well that we were leaving the island soon.

GOODBYE

When *Henry David Thoreau* left his cabin at Walden Pond in the fall of 1847, he wrote in his journal, "Perhaps if I lived there much longer, I might live there forever. One would think twice before he accepted heaven on such terms." It's as good an explanation as any for why we went away.

I had come to the island planning to stay for a year. Our resident's permit allowed us to stay until early June. Our airline tickets were open-ended but the time was coming when we would have to set a departure date and so I began to go through the motions of getting ready to leave. I packed up boxes of books and papers and shipped them out on the boat, fairly certain I would never see them again. I made arrangements to return our rental car and be defrauded out of our deposit. I started giving away our possessions to friends—our little radio to Mata, the boys' clothes to friends with smaller children, our big flashlight to Emily, some books we would never read again to the library, the perfect crab shell I found on the beach to Nate Flynn.

But the whole time I sorted and shipped and packed it seemed only a game, like playing dress-up and drinking invisible tea at a pretend tea party. No matter how diligently one goes through the motions, it doesn't make the game real.

Friday, May 16
> *The boys and I went to the airport today and changed our open-ended tickets for tickets with a firm departure date on them. Coming out of the ticket office, next to the coconut trees with the tiny red baby coconuts growing in clusters, I thought I would cry.*

My status on the island had evolved. I had become known as the woman who was "interested in things", so friends of Emily's would come, shyly at first but then less so, and bring me things they had pulled out of their attics, relics from the old way of life, or stories that their grandparents had told them, or special fruit from their gardens. Emily would announce their arrival, saying she had told so-and-so that I was "interested in things" and they wondered if I had ever seen such a flower, or heard a certain story. I still have the photographs I made then, of delicate blossoms cradled in wrinkled hands. And in my field journal are transcriptions of stories they had been waiting so long for someone to listen to again. As it became known that I was going away, more and more people came, giving their memories into my care.

I had unintentionally become a connoisseur of flowers and fruit, even of coconuts. One day Lena brought me an uto, a special kind of sprouted coconut, because I had mentioned that I had never tasted one. Mata whacked it open with her machete and we sat on the veranda eating the inside, which was crispy and delicate and sweet. The best ones, Lena said, came from the island of Pukapuka where they buried the coconuts until the nuts sprouted, which made them sweeter. We became uto snobs, preferring the ones from Pukapuka, although we had never tasted them.

The drinking coconuts, nu, were the immature ones. They were called green, but they came in lots of colors: brown, yellow and orange as well as green. I bought them by the dozen in the market, lifting each one to make sure it felt heavy so I knew it would have lots of juice. The coconuts were husked already, so I just had to poke a hole through one of their eyes and we could drink the juice with straws. (I was afraid to open them with a machete as

Mata did; I would have put the chances of my cutting off my hand at about fifty:fifty.)

Sometimes kids would be selling nu by the side of the road and I would stop and buy them, one dollar for a small one, two for a large one, and three for a whopper. Once I saw Fiona's son Oskar walking down the road in Arorangi and stopped to give him a lift back home, but he could barely squeeze in because our car seat was piled so high with coconuts.

"Um," he said, pulling his knees up under his chin and searching for something polite to say, "are all of these for you?"

We knew about bananas too. There were different sizes—Tris liked the little finger bananas—and colours, such as the wild red ones that grew only in the interior; you had to know somebody who would go and pick them for you. I asked Emily and Lena and Mata over and over, "What is this one called? And this one?" They would tell me in Māori, and spell it for me. I wrote down all the names, along with the descriptions and the fine distinctions.

The two kids who worked at the post office knew I was leaving because I went in every few days with another box packed up with things to ship to myself at my address in the US. They promised to forward on any mail that arrived for me after I had left the island. Needless to say, I never got a thing.

Wednesday, May 21
Kia orana everyone,

I hope you are all doing well. Thank you for all the letters and care packages you have been sending. It has made the three of us feel very good to know we have not been forgotten. I wanted to let you all know, however, that it is time to stop. Anything sent now will not get here before we leave.

It is inconceivable to me that soon we will not live here anymore—that I will park my car without looking up first to do a coconut check, and wake up without a cranky rooster to help me do it. It is inconceivable that we will again be required to wear shoes in supermarkets and restaurants, and that it will get cold enough to wear long pants. It is hard to picture a world where women don't wear wreathes of flowers in their hair and where men, when they want to look nice, don't tuck wild gardenia blossoms behind their ears. And I wonder if white people will seem very small to me, the way that Polynesians once seemed so big?

What will it be like to drive on a road that doesn't border a lagoon of shattered blue? There is a place here where the road winds through a bit of littoral forest and then emerges to a turquoise expanse of bay that still leaves me dazzled every time, even after all these months of coming upon it almost daily. I often think—when capable of coherent thought at all—of the beginning of Finnegans Wake: "riverrun past Eve and Adam's, from swerve of shore to bend of bay". Guava and lime will not litter the yard any more and crabs won't scuttle around in the kitchen. I know intellectually that these things are true, but in my heart I don't really believe it.

Aiden and Tris are doing well and have grown out of half of their clothes and shredded the rest. We have found some riding stables with very tame horses on the other side of the island; the boys like to go riding, and take the horses splashing out into the lagoon halfway to the reef. Then they ride back to shore and gallop across the sand and through the palm groves and thickets of hibiscus back to the stable. I don't think they quite understand that they will not always live like this.

Emily seems quite sad that we are going and keeps asking me when we will be coming back home, by which she means her house. The way to say "soon" in Māori is "Kare e rou atu te tuatau kua aravei akaou"—"The time is not long that we will meet again."

"There is always a place for you all back here at home," Emily says. Somerset Maugham said that if you ever go to the South Seas, you shouldn't leave; if

you leave, you will spend the rest of your life trying to
get back. My friend Bill, however, sends the following
line from Goethe: "No one walks under the palm trees
unpunished."

Take care, everyone. The time is not long that we
will meet again.

Ka kite! Kathy

Aiden's eighth birthday was on a Sunday at the end of May. I ordered a chocolate cake from the T-Shayla-J Bakery, but in the middle of Saturday night I suddenly woke and sat up straight in bed with the realisation that I had forgotten to pick up the cake. And of course the bakery was not open on Sundays. We didn't even have the ingredients at home to make a cake for him, poor kid. Sometimes the idea of stores being open on Sunday seems especially good.

Aiden took the lack of a cake pretty well, especially since he wasn't getting presents either. I had convinced him to wait until we got back to the US, where there were, you know, *stores*. He had wanted to have a last horseback ride, so at least he got to do that. It was cloudy but the rain miraculously held off. On DJ, his favourite horse, he careened madly past me on the beach, with Tris hot on his tail. As I watched them plunge into the palm grove, I feebly called out "Hold on! Hold *on*!" after them.

Faintly in the distance I heard Aiden's voice yelling, "Yee *haw!*"

I went to the bakery first thing Monday morning to see if the cake was still there, but Shayla had taken it home and her kids had eaten it.

"You should have called me," she said.

"I didn't know your number," I said.

"You could have asked anybody," she said. This was true. I could probably have dialled random telephone numbers and hit a cousin in three tries at most.

I dreamed one night that it snowed. I was walking from Tupapa to Taputapuatea and the road was covered over with grass. The grass turned to frost and then I noticed it was snowing. I stopped at the café across from Ted's house and it was coming down hard. Then the café was at Carr Mill and I was back in graduate school in North Carolina.

The ancestors now knew that we were leaving and began to say good-bye. One night, very late, I woke up. The glass slats on the window above my bed were sparkling with tiny golden lights, dancing in a shimmering cascade. At first I didn't know it was the ancestors. I thought, "How strange. There must be lots of cars with their headlights on going home late along the beach road. Or maybe the moonlight is coming through the leaves of the tipani trees."

The lights snapped and fizzed along the edge of the glass. The wind was warm, and thinking the stars might be out I went silently on to the veranda, leaving behind the sounds of the boys breathing deeply, cuddled together in their sleep. The moon must be very low, I thought, just above the dark horizon of the sea.

From the veranda, however, the lights seemed to be coming from inside our room. The beach road was silent and deserted and I couldn't see the moon. I went back in and the lights seemed to be coming from outside again. I put my face close to the glass of the windows. The lights glittered in their depths.

I went outside again and sat for a long time on the veranda steps, watching the clouds come and go between the palm trees and the stars of the Southern Cross. Then I went inside, lay in bed and watched the ancestors play above my head. Sometime in the early morning I fell asleep.

Later I told Emily about the lights. We were sitting in our usual places, on the side of the house facing east. "It's the ancestors," she said, in a way that convinced me it was true beyond doubt. Her eyes filled with tears. "They're saying goodbye to you."

I am back home now—or rather I am back in the house that I own. I don't know when I will ever be *home* again. Maybe home is a time that you live through, and all you can do when that time is over is carry it with you, inside you, for the rest of your life.

Lots of our friends came, on our last night on the island, to eat and drink with us while we waited late into the night for the time to go to the airport for the flight to Tahiti and then on to Los Angeles. For a while, we ate and laughed. Nate Flynn backed his truck up to the veranda, turned on the tape player and danced me back and forth across the front of the house, wrapping me close in his arms. Ted drew me a picture of a dark moon over the sea. Elise made me an 'ei katu of delicate wooden flowers to wear on the plane. Mata brought gifts for us all and everyone heaped us with 'ei pupu, the shell necklaces given to departing loved ones.

But after a while it was time to leave. Everyone but Emily and Lena was going to the airport. Emily and I held each other for a long time. "I am your mother," she whispered over and over again into my hair. "I am your mother." Lena stayed behind to put her to bed.

At the airport, we stopped to see Rosa at the bank window—it was her night to work the money exchange—then we went all together in a big mob through ticketing and baggage check-in. Finally, though, Aiden and Tris and I had to say good-bye and go through security by ourselves. I could see Mata until the very last, standing in front of the crowd, smiling and crying both at the same time.

Nga's husband was running the X-ray machine and he wished us goodbye from Nga: she was home with a bad cold, but had told him to watch for us coming through. In the departure lounge we sat near Jake Numanga, our cousin now, while he played his ukulele for the departing tourists. The young woman from the little CITC souvenir shop in the departure area abandoned it and came to sit with us. Because she worked in the main CITC on weekdays, the boys and I knew her, even though we didn't know her name.

"Are you going on a trip?" she asked.

"No," I said, "we have to go back to live in the US now."

"Oh, that's too bad," she said, looking sad for us. "When will you be back?"

"Christmas," I said, knowing it wasn't true. "We will be back at Christmas."

After she went back to the shop, I held sleepy Tris and Aiden, one on either side of me, and waited to board the plane. The tourists looked strange, sitting there not connected to anyone. That's how we had been when we first came—disconnected, all alone with only each other under the wide, empty sky.

EPILOGUE

Friday, July 18
Kia orana everyone,

We've arrived back in the US—twice, in fact. The culture shock has been, well, shocking. The traffic noise from Boulder Street seems deafening and we are so unaccustomed to air pollution that coming in from the airport I was quite certain the car was on fire.

Aiden and Tris seem to have taken things in their stride, but I have suffered rather dramatically from capitalism overload. The grocery store was especially bewildering—a hundred different varieties of salsa, and homeless people sleeping in the rain on the sidewalk outside. I was so dazed by it all that now my underarms smell brisk and manly and the children are brushing their teeth with denture cream. We used to make sure to stock up on toilet paper whenever the toilet paper boat came in. Now we can get toilet paper that advertises itself as having "Aloe and Vitamin E" and "Extra Wide Ridges"—an unfortunate mental connection with Ruffles Potato Chips that has put me off bean dip for life.

I have only recently begun driving again. I had to first conquer a reflex to close my eyes and scream whenever anyone made a right-hand turn into what my spinal cord thinks will be oncoming traffic. The existence of other drivers keeps me in the right lane, but I am on my own inside the car, where everything is backwards. I've stopped getting in through the passenger door, but I still have a tendency to put on the windshield wipers to indicate I'm turning.

It seems strange to park without looking up first to do a coconut check, and there are little things all the time that I miss. It seems strange that there are so few flowers and so many shoes. It seems very strange that there are so many white people everywhere. And although clean running water is miraculous, I can't stop regretting the loss of our dazzling turquoise lagoon. I unconsciously look for it and then get a sinking feeling when I realise it is a very long way away.

We left almost immediately to visit Jonathan in Zürich, which is almost, but not quite, exactly the furthest point on the planet from Rarotonga. We may have gone a little too far too fast to fully assimilate the Swiss experience. After a week, Tris asked me which was the streetcar "that goes all around this island".

Of course, he also thought a newsstand in LA airport
was a church—it seemed so big and glittering that he
could come up with no other rational explanation
*   I hope that you are all doing well. Take care.*

Kia manuia, Kathy

A year after we left Rarotonga, Aiden, Tris and I went to
live in Switzerland. In the middle of a dreary dingy snowy
February, Jonathan and I were married in a little castle on
the shores of the Greifensee. Fiona, Oskar and Alma came
over from England to be with us, and Jonathan's parents
came from New Jersey. My father had suffered a sudden
stroke the month before and wasn't able to make the flight.

I spent most of the day in a daze, except for the part
where I was having a panic attack. Fiona valiantly got me
dressed and encouraged me to breathe deeply. "That's not
breathing, darling," she said to me at one point. "That's
gasping."

The boys were sweet and supportive. They stood with
Fiona next to me during the ceremony and winked when
I looked at them. I could still fit into the dress I had
bought several months before in a tiny shop in Carr Mill,
North Carolina, which was surprising, given that I had
comforted myself in the grey Swiss winter by baking and
helping to eat five apple pies in the three weeks leading up
to the wedding.

We were married by an impersonal justice of the peace from Volketswil. I have no recollection of what she said, other than that at one point she showed us a thick yellow book about the same size as *The Brothers Karamazov*; apparently it is the rule book for Swiss marriages. I tried hard to look as though I were paying attention—something I am good at because I used to practise it in faculty meetings. I didn't dare glance at Jonathan for fear I would dissolve in uncontrollable laughter.

After eighteen months, we fled back to the US. Now we live again in Colorado, where it never rains in summer and where a sickly withered pawpaw, imported from Honduras, costs seven dollars at the grocery store. Jonathan still makes me dizzy, Aiden and Tris still live in a magical world, and the wind blows hard almost every day. We have paintings by Nate Flynn hanging on our walls, and two of Fiona's photographs. We have yet to see ghosts, but we keep hoping.

I got a letter from Emily last week. "Thank you so much for the boys' photos," she writes. "My word, they are growing so much since last I saw them. I am so glad that you are all well and that you are all happy. Mata said that she would call by to see the boys' photos. I am still wearing the flip-flop sandals you left behind. Each time I wear them that lovely thought of you flows back. Well, maybe one day we will meet again."

ACKNOWLEDGEMENTS

When I returned from Rarotonga, the first book I wrote was *Collective Creativity*, a scholarly work on the art world of the Cook Islands. That *An Afternoon in Summer* now exists certainly supports the thesis of that book: this has been a collective endeavour from the very beginning, and would not have been possible without the help and support of numerous people.

I would like to start by thanking Emily and Mata, two beautiful, generous Rarotongan women who provided my children and me with care and support every day of our time on the island. This book was written with great love for them both and recounts only a small part of the joys they gave to Aiden, Tris and me. I would also like to thank the many other people on the island, some of whom are mentioned in these pages and some of whom are not, who made our lives so intensely happy.

During the writing of *An Afternoon in Summer*, my two amazing friends, Amy Fusselman and Fiona Haser, gave me not only support and encouragement but the invaluable gift of honest (if gentle) critical feedback. Without friends willing to undertake such a difficult task, no book could be written. I am lucky to have them both in my life.

My agent, P. J. Mark, has been incredibly kind and supportive. His constant generosity has been remarkable and I thank him from the bottom of my heart for that.

At Awa Press, Mary Varnham has worked unbelievably hard on this text and taken considerable care with it. I very much appreciate not only her patient and indefatigable labour, but her willingness to take a risk on the book in the first place.

I am fortunate to be surrounded by a loving and supportive family, all of whom in innumerable ways have helped bring this book into being, but it is my husband, Jonathan Poritz, who has in ways big and small, too numerous to count, over years now, truly made it possible. My gratitude and love for him go beyond any words that I could write.